D1011520

More Praise for Mike Myatt's
Hacking Leadership

"Great leaders are aware of gaps and blind spots in their organizations, teams, and lives. Learn the secrets of great leaders when you read Mike Myatt's *Hacking Leadership*!"

—Marshall Goldsmith,
2 million-selling author of the *New York Times* bestsellers,
MOJO and *What Got You Here Won't Get You There*

"*Hacking Leadership* is a thought-provoking, status-quo-shattering jolt of leadership wisdom that can propel anyone in the direction of their full leadership potential. At a time when scores of people are content settling for *What Is*, Mike challenges us to ask ourselves, *What If?* Instead of simply writing another book on leadership, he's penned a powerfully persuasive narrative that reminds us the only limits to our leadership are those we impose on ourselves. *Hacking Leadership* is a must read for everyone!"

—Brigadier General John E. Michel,
Commanding General NATO Air Training Command-Afghanistan,
and author of *(No More) Mediocre Me: How Saying No
to the Status Quo Will Propel You From Ordinary to Extraordinary*

"*Hacking Leadership* merits a place on every twenty-first century leader's short list of must-read books. Written from the heart and the mind of the renowned leadership expert Mike Myatt, this remarkable manual for action will inspire you to the greatest leadership contribution in your work and life."

—James Strock, author, *Serve to Lead,
Theodore Roosevelt on Leadership, Reagan on Leadership,*
former George H.W. Bush appointee
as chief law enforcement officer for the U.S. EPA

"Mike's insights are logical, entertaining and well outlined. Deep experience with a myriad of leaders enables him to understand the landscape, and his passionate pursuit of innovation lets him crack it open. *Hacking Leadership* is a fresh take on what it means to be an effective leader and take action."

—**Thomas X. Geisel**, CEO, Sun Bancorp, Inc.

"Every leader I know, including myself, has leadership gaps, and all of us need a resource and framework for not only identifying the gaps, but also a practical roadmap to help close those gaps. *Hacking Leadership* is an essential tool for every leader to have in their toolbox for working on their own leadership and thus improving the team and overall organization. Mike reminds us all not to settle for the status quo, and the important role each of us has to bring about the change we seek. True leaders do something about it, and are willing to mix things up and hack away at their leadership, with the constant pursuit of excellence and thus their true leadership potential."

—**Brad Lomenick**, president and key visionary, Catalyst, author, *The Catalyst Leader*

Hacking
Leadership

Hacking Leadership

The 11 Gaps Every Business Needs to Close and the Secrets to Closing Them Quickly

Mike Myatt

WILEY

Cover image: © iStockphoto.com/ROMAOSLO
Cover design: Wiley

Copyright © 2014 by Mike Myatt. All rights reserved.

Published by John Wiley & Sons, Inc., Hoboken, New Jersey.
Published simultaneously in Canada.

No part of this publication may be reproduced, stored in a retrieval system, or transmitted
in any form or by any means, electronic, mechanical, photocopying, recording, scanning,
or otherwise, except as permitted under Section 107 or 108 of the 1976 United
States Copyright Act, without either the prior written permission of the Publisher,
or authorization through payment of the appropriate per-copy fee to the Copyright
Clearance Center, Inc., 222 Rosewood Drive, Danvers, MA 01923, (978) 750-8400, fax
(978) 646-8600, or on the Web at www.copyright.com. Requests to the Publisher for
permission should be addressed to the Permissions Department, John Wiley & Sons, Inc.,
111 River Street, Hoboken, NJ 07030, (201) 748-6011, fax (201) 748-6008, or online at
www.wiley.com/go/permissions.

Limit of Liability/Disclaimer of Warranty: While the publisher and author have used their
best efforts in preparing this book, they make no representations or warranties with respect
to the accuracy or completeness of the contents of this book and specifically disclaim any
implied warranties of merchantability or fitness for a particular purpose. No warranty
may be created or extended by sales representatives or written sales materials. The advice
and strategies contained herein may not be suitable for your situation. You should consult
with a professional where appropriate. Neither the publisher nor author shall be liable for
any loss of profit or any other commercial damages, including but not limited to special,
incidental, consequential, or other damages.

For general information on our other products and services or for technical support, please
contact our Customer Care Department within the United States at (800) 762-2974,
outside the United States at (317) 572-3993 or fax (317) 572-4002.

Wiley publishes in a variety of print and electronic formats and by print-on-demand.
Some material included with standard print versions of this book may not be included in
e-books or in print-on-demand. If this book refers to media such as a CD or DVD that
is not included in the version you purchased, you may download this material at http://
booksupport.wiley.com. For more information about Wiley products, visit www.wiley.com.

Library of Congress Cataloging-in-Publication Data:

ISBN 978-1-118-81741-4 (Hardcover)
ISBN 978-1-118-81737-7 (ePDF)
ISBN 978-1-118-81735-3 (ePub)

Printed in the United States of America

10 9 8 7 6 5 4 3 2 1

To my family—they inspire me to be better.
To my friends—they challenge me to do better.
To my clients—they require me to think better.
To my co-workers—they motivate me to lead better.

Contents

Prologue

I n my office hangs a plaque given to me as a gift. It originally read, *It Is What It Is*. After a few weeks of reading that phrase several times a day, what I once regarded as a harmless saying began to challenge my thinking and poke at my convictions. It became clear to me this seemingly innocent phrase embodied much of what's wrong with leadership today. So I did what any good leader would do—I took action.

I rummaged through my desk drawer and found my whittling knife. I then proceeded to carve the following inscription beneath the original statement: *Until You Decide To Change It*. What once served as a statement of defeat now reads as instructive encouragement; the text no longer lulls people who read it into a state of complacency—it now propels them forward.

This simple piece of wall art (prior to my modification) is sadly representative of many who hold positions of leadership. Burdened by common practice, busyness, and an aversion to change, many leaders today suffer from an acute case of mental numbness. They have fallen prey to the slow seduction of the status quo. As time has passed, they have succumbed to accepting *what is* instead of pursuing *what if*. They make safe choices instead of smart choices—they have forgotten what it is to be a leader.

There is no shortage of debate surrounding leadership when it comes to philosophy, style, definitional distinctions, nuances, complex theory, and so and so forth. That said, I believe most reasonable people would agree leadership is nothing if not personal. Leadership can represent a pursuit, discipline, practice, passion, calling, skill, competency, obligation, duty, compulsion, or even an obsession. I've known those who have worshiped at the altar of leadership as a religion, and a bit of reflection will reveal more than a few leadership revolutions dotting the historical timeline. My goal for *Hacking Leadership* is to challenge your thinking and your perceptions with regard to the state of leadership. So, my question is this; what's next for leadership?

In my first book *Leadership Matters* (2007), I made the following statement:

> Whether through malice or naiveté, those who trivialize the value of leadership place us all at risk. Poor leadership cripples businesses, ruins economies, destroys families, loses wars, and can bring the demise of nations—Leadership Matters.

On an individual basis, a person's perceived leadership ability, or lack thereof, will in large part determine their station in life; the schools they're admitted to, the jobs they hold, the family life they create, the influence they acquire, and the financial security they achieve. On a collective basis, the quality of leadership has a ripple effect (positive or negative) that can impact generations. Leadership, good or bad, is a contagion.

Nothing impacts our world like leadership, and sadly, the practice of leadership is broken. We live in a society where the pace of change has never been faster and more dramatic, yet our leadership practices have remained painfully stagnant. Using eighteenth, nineteenth, or twentieth-century leadership practices in the twenty-first century simply doesn't work. It's time for a fresh perspective—it's time to begin Hacking Leadership.

Core leadership principles have remained largely the same since the dawn of time. The problem with today's leaders is they don't understand how to integrate time-tested principles with evolving leadership practices built for twenty-first century success. The world in which *you* attempt to implement previously successful strategies and tactics has changed and is ever changing. Organizations, their employees, and the various constituencies they serve are far different today from what they were centuries, decades, or even a few years ago.

Here's the thing—these core leadership principles need not be abandoned, but outdated and ill conceived practices must be hacked in order to reestablish leadership equilibrium. *Hacking Leadership* puts the practice of leadership under a transformative lens for the purpose simplifying the complex, while not throwing the baby out with the bathwater.

It's important for leaders to embrace the practice of change as it applies to their own tradecraft. I've spent much of my adult life committed to the belief and practice there is always room for innovation, development, and improvement. As much as some don't want to hear it, this applies to leadership as well. When leaders hold themselves to a higher standard of rigor, discipline, accountability, and transparency everyone wins.

I've often said the rigidity of a closed mind is the first step in limiting opportunity. So let me ask you this question: When was the last time *you* changed something about *you*? Not someone or something else, but *your* thinking, *your* philosophy, *your* vision, *your* approach, *your* attitude, or *your* development. Most leaders are quite skilled at embracing change—except when the focus of the change initiative happens to be on them. Show me a person that never changes their mind, and I'll show you a static thinker who has sentenced their mind to a prison of mediocrity and wasted potential.

Smart leaders challenge everything—especially conventional thought, best practices, and dominant logic. When I refer to dominant logic, I'm referencing existing behaviors/practices, which lock organizations into a pattern of once-productive thinking that no longer is (false truths held as real). Anything in business can be improved, everything can be reimagined, and many things can flat-out be eliminated. The trick is knowing what items to focus on—which items to hack.

I want to pause here and set the tone moving forward by giving you my definition of hacking:

hacking [hak-ing]—present participle of hack (verb) to discover an alternate path, clever and skillful tricks, shortcuts and workarounds, breaking the code, deciphering complexity, influencing outcomes, acquiring access, creating innovative customizations to existing/outdated methodologies.

Everyone has blind spots, and leadership gaps exist in every organization. The purpose of this book is to equip leaders at every level with an actionable framework to identify blind spots and close leadership gaps. *Hacking Leadership* offers a fresh perspective that will make it easy for leaders to create a road map to identify, refine, develop, and achieve their true leadership potential.

Hackers are innovative thinkers who acquire and distribute knowledge, tips, and tricks for solving complex problems—they reinvent strategies, protocols, and practices to create more effective solutions to both existing problems and new challenges. They adopt the mind-set of innovating around best practices in pursuit of next practices.

Most of us are all too familiar with the statement "you don't know what you don't know"—there's never been a more dangerous cop-out for leaders than rationalizing ignorance. The fact of the matter is the best leaders are poignantly aware of what they don't know, and exhaust all efforts to close those knowledge gaps.

In many respects, leadership is nothing more than identifying personal, team, organizational, and market blind spots and then dealing with them in the most effective fashion. Therefore it's critically important for leaders to understand that most blind spots exist in the form of gaps—positional gaps, philosophical gaps, strategic gaps, operational gaps, expectation gaps, knowledge gaps, and so on. Gaps exist in every organization: The issue is whether you recognize them, and if so, how you choose to deal with them.

Many leaders choose to be ignorant of gaps and pretend they don't exist. The problem is that when leaders fall into a gap, it often resembles a crevasse from which there is no escape. Smart leaders proactively seek out gaps in an effort to bridge, close, fill, jump, or navigate around whatever chasm they happen to be facing. The better you become at turning gaps into opportunities (hacking the gaps), the better leader you'll become.

I've had the privilege of working with thousands of leaders around the globe. I'm honored to count among my clients many past and present chairmen and CEOs of some of the world's leading organizations. What these men and women have consistently taught me is that holding a position of leadership is not the same thing as being a good leader; understanding the basic tenants of leadership is not the same thing as being able to successfully apply them, and that leadership isn't a destination it's a journey.

While many things can cause leaders to stumble, I've found there are 11 specific leadership gaps, which if not properly identified, understood, and addressed can be fatal. In each of the 11 chapters that follow, I address a particular topic by framing it within the context of a leadership gap. I then go on to offer a series of hacks to help you reframe your thinking so that you can either avoid or altogether eliminate the gap.

Finally, I want to share with you my opinions and biases about most business books, as well as offer a few insights for how you can get the most out of this work. Most business books are full of fluff, and while they may be entertaining, they often serve no real purpose other than to transfer some of your wealth to the author. In the final analysis, a book is only as valuable to leaders as their willingness to discerningly pull the useful concepts off the pages and place them into practice. Books are little more than words on a page unless *you* choose to make them something more.

I would certainly encourage you to challenge the concepts put forth in this book. More importantly, I would encourage you to challenge your own thinking. Don't just read the book; study the material and commit to becoming a better leader. The day you stop hacking leadership is the day you should stop leading. Good luck and good hacking. . . .

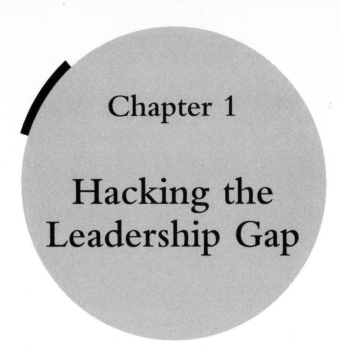

Chapter 1

Hacking the Leadership Gap

*The plausibility of impossibility only becomes
a probability in the absence of leadership.*

Overview—The Commoditization of Leadership

Whether you believe leadership has evolved or devolved over time,
there is no disputing the practice of leadership has become a conten-
tious topic steeped in ethereal, ambiguous rhetoric. Everyone seems to
have an opinion of what constitutes good leadership, but if good leadership is so easy to define and identify, why then does it seem so hard
to come by?

Society has essentially commoditized leadership resulting in a leadership bubble of sorts. Because leadership has become the latest version
of an entitlement program, too many unqualified leaders have been
allowed to enter the ranks.

This is not just a business problem—it's a global leadership problem. The media is littered with daily examples of those placed in positions of leadership who failed to lead. Leaders are often selected, promoted, and retained on entirely the wrong basis. When leadership is perceived as little more than a title granting access to a platform for personal gain, rather than a privilege resulting in an opportunity to serve, we'll continue to find ourselves in a crisis of leadership.

Those of you familiar with my work know I'm a dyed in the wool leadership guy. . . . I believe all things begin and end with leadership. In fact, I hold this thesis so dear, I've said for years "businesses don't fail, projects don't fail, and products don't fail—leaders fail."

With principled, effective leadership, all things are possible. It's only when optics become more important than ethics, when profit becomes more important than purpose, when process becomes more important than people, and when politics becomes more important than doing the right thing, that individuals and organizations lose their direction. Sadly, this is where much of the world finds itself today. The good news is by hacking current leadership frameworks and dynamics we can find our way back to true north.

The best leaders understand leadership is the key to unlocking and realizing limitless potential. I want you to think about leadership like this—the only boarders to leadership are those which are self-imposed. The only limits on your personal, team, or organizational leadership are the ones you submit to.

So, you have a choice—you can limit your worldview, or you can expand it—you can embrace the status quo, or you can shatter it—you can follow *best* practices, or you can lead innovation around them to identify *next* practices. Real leaders don't limit themselves, but more importantly they refuse to limit those they lead.

All truly great leaders I've had the opportunity to work with have had one thing in common—they have a clear understanding of their strengths and weaknesses. They've learned to check their ego, enhance their level of self-awareness, and understand how others perceive them. They are clear thinkers who understand their role and are prepared to act accordingly.

This is a foundational chapter—one that sets the tone you can build upon chapter by chapter as you move forward. Therefore, the balance of this chapter will offer some insights into how you can hack away at the self-rationalizations and justifications keeping you from reaching your leadership potential.

The Leadership Gap Defined

Those who become what they do not understand will not like the outcome. It's imperative you define yourself on both an aspirational and practical level as a leader in order to lead well. Leadership isn't just a role or a title—it's a choice. The best leaders choose to be better, they choose to be different—they choose to lead well. The seminal question you must ask yourself as a leader is why should anyone be led by you?

Think about it like this—aside from having a job, how are people better off for being led by you? In order to consistently receive the right answer to the aforementioned question, a leader must first gain an understanding of the following three critical leadership gaps:

1. **The Development Gap:** This refers to the gap between how you assess your current leadership ability and your true potential as a leader. An accurate understanding of this gap indicates whether you see leadership as a destination or as a continuum. It will determine whether you grow and develop your leadership skills, or whether you will follow the path of least resistance and rest upon your laurels. Keep this in mind—it is impossible for a leader who is not growing and developing to lead a growing and developing enterprise.

2. **The Influence Gap:** While influence can be generated in all directions, for purposes of this discussion I'm referring to the gap between your self-assessment and the assessment of your leadership ability by your peers. Your understanding of this gap, and willingness to do something about it, will determine your ability to build a cohesive team. Leaders who don't have the trust and respect of their team won't be able to generate the influence necessary to perform at the expected levels.

3. **The Reality Gap:** This refers to the difference between how you view yourself and how those you lead feel about you. A leader who loses the faith and confidence of their workforce won't be able to attract and retain talent, will have a culture on life support, and sub-par performance that ensures only one thing—a limited shelf life.

Let's stop right here and do a quick gut check. I want you to rate yourself as a leader on a scale from 1 to 10, with 1 representing the worst in leadership and 10 being the best in leadership. I don't want you to rate your leadership potential, but rather how you are currently performing as a leader. This is a risk-free evaluation, as nobody will see your score but you; do this now and write the number here ____.

Here's what we know to be true based upon the empirical evidence gleaned from conducting thousands of interviews with senior executives. Regardless of your position/title, you likely rated yourself between a 6 and an 8. Am I right? The reality is regardless of how transparent you tried to be, 90+ percent of all people in leadership positions won't rate themselves below a 6. Similarly, 90+ percent of people in leadership positions won't rate themselves higher than an 8.

While this first set of data might not shock you, here's something else we know about leadership self-evaluations—leaders consistently overrate themselves. How do we know this? Because we have also surveyed thousands of subordinates and peers, as well as those whom the leaders report to. This next set of data will shock you.

When we ask those who work for and with you to rate you on the same scale with which you conducted your self-assessment, they rate you on average 200 basis points lower than you rate yourself—that's right, two full percentage points lower. So, if you rated yourself an 8 your co-workers likely rate you a 6. If you rated yourself a 6, then they likely rated you a 4. How does that make you feel?

The difference between your self-assessment score and how others rate you is what I refer to as the leadership gap. Whether the leadership gap is perception or reality doesn't really matter—it's nonetheless the gap all leaders must learn to hack.

Put yourself in the shoes of those who rated you—how impassioned and motivated would you be to awaken each morning to go to work for a leader who rates somewhere between a 4 and 6?

Where leadership always runs amok is when hubris overshadows humility, and self-serving motives take the place of service beyond self. Leadership is not about the power and the accolades bestowed upon the leader; it's about the betterment of those whom the leader serves. At its essence, leadership is about people. At its core, leadership is about improving the status quo, inspiring positive change, and challenging conventional thinking.

As long as positional and philosophical arguments are more important than forward progress, as long as being right is esteemed above being vulnerable and open to new thought, as long as ego is elevated above empathy and compassion, as long as rhetoric holds more value than performance, and as long as we tolerate these things as acceptable behavior we will all suffer at the hands of poor leadership.

I think most of us understand at a high level that companies live and die by the quality of their leadership—but how many of you really internalize this deep down at a personal level? If you're ready to dig deep and get serious about leadership, the first thing to understand is how control limits your ability to lead.

Hacking the Control Gap

The most common mistake I see leaders make is to attempt to lead through control. As counterintuitive as it might seem, in order to gain influence you must surrender control. The reality is you'll rarely encounter the words *leadership* and *surrender* used together in complementary fashion. Society has labeled surrender as a sign of leadership weakness, when in fact it can be among the greatest of leadership strengths. Leaders who fail to learn how to hack the control gap fail to lead up to their potential.

Let me be clear, I'm not encouraging giving in or giving up—I am suggesting you learn the ever so subtle art of letting go. Leaders simply operate at their best when they understand their ability to influence is much more fruitful than their ability to control. Here's the thing—the purpose of leadership is not to shine the spotlight on yourself, but to unlock the potential of others so they can in turn shine the spotlight on countless more. Control is about power—not leadership. Surrender allows leaders to stop impeding themselves and focus on adding value to those whom they serve.

If you're still not convinced the art of leadership is learning that the focus point should be on surrender not control, consider this: Control restricts potential, limits initiative, and inhibits talent. Surrender fosters collaboration, encourages innovation, and enables possibility. Controlling leaders create bottlenecks rather than increase throughput. They signal a lack of trust and confidence and often come across as insensitive if not arrogant. When you experience weak teams, micro-management, frequent turf wars, high stress, operational strain, and a culture of fear, you are experiencing what control has to offer—not very attractive is it?

Surrender allows the savvy leader to serve, but control demands that the egocentric leader be served. Surrender allows leadership to scale and a culture of leadership to be established. Surrender prefers loose collaborative networks to rigid hierarchical structures allowing information to be more readily shared and distributed. Leaders who understand surrender think community, ecosystem, and culture—not org chart. Surrender is what not only allows the dots to be connected, but it's what allows the dots to be multiplied. Controlling leaders operate in a world of addition and subtraction, while the calculus of a leader who understands surrender is built on exponential multiplication.

I have found those who embrace control are simply attempting to consolidate power, while those who practice surrender are facilitating the distribution of authority. When what you seek is to build into others more than glorifying self, you have developed a level of leadership maturity that values surrender over control. Surrender is the mind-set that creates the desire for leaders to give credit rather than take it, to prefer hearing over being heard, to dialogue instead of monologue, to have an open mind over a closed mind, to value unlearning as much as learning. Control messages selfishness, while surrender conveys self-lessness—which is more important to you?

Keep this in mind—we all surrender, but not all surrender is honorable. Some surrender to their ego, to the wrong priorities, or to other distractive habits. Others surrender to the positive realization that they are not the center of the universe—they surrender to something beyond themselves in order to accomplish more for others. Bottom line—what you do or don't surrender to will define you. Assuming you surrender to the right things, surrender is not a sign of leadership weakness, but is perhaps the ultimate sign of leadership confidence. I'll leave you with this quote from William Booth: "The greatness of a man's power is the measure of his surrender."

Once you recognize where you stand with regard to the leadership gap and you get past limiting control issues, it's time to identify your blind spots. This requires deep introspection and a heightened sense of self-awareness.

The Awareness Gap—Finding the Blind Spots

Leader Beware—ignorant bliss, no matter how enjoyable, is still ignorant. If you're in a position of leadership and don't feel you have any blind spots, you're either very naïve or very arrogant. All leaders have blind spots—the question is what are they doing about them? The reality is most leaders invest so much time assessing the cultural and functional dynamics of their organizations that they often forget the importance of critically assessing themselves—big mistake.

I've never understood leaders who make heavy investments in personal and professional development early in their careers, who then go on to make only minimal investments in learning once they have reached the C-suite. Learning and development are lifelong endeavors.

The learning journey doesn't come to an end just because you reach a certain station in life—or at least it shouldn't. It has consistently been my experience that leaders who are not growing simply cannot lead growing organizations. Moreover, leaders who fail to continue developing will always be replaced by those who do. A leader who fails to understand the value of self-awareness fails to understand their true potential as a leader.

The further up the ladder leaders climb, the more they must be on top of their game as they have the broadest sphere of influence, the largest ability to impact a business, and they also now have the most at risk. It is at this place leaders should make the heaviest investment in refining their game, because increased performance will pay the biggest dividends. Let me be as clear as I can—the more responsibility leaders have, the bigger their obligation to be on the forward edge of learning, growth, and development.

The ancient Greek philosopher Socrates had a few guiding principles that today's leaders would do well to adopt: Socrates said, "Know Thyself" and "An unexamined life is not worth living." Those leaders who actively pursue gaining a better understanding of themselves will not only reduce their number of blind spots, but they'll also find developing a sense of awareness is the key to increasing emotional intelligence. The better you know yourself, the more effective you'll be, and the better you'll relate to others.

To build on the hacks covered thus far, it will be important to evolve your critical thinking. This is best done through the refining lens of extreme clarity.

The Key to Clarity—White Space

Here's something you may not want to hear, but you should definitely take to heart; if you're having difficulty ordering your world, it's nobody's fault but yours. I don't care how busy you are, but I do care about what you accomplish—the former doesn't always lead to the latter. Busy leaders are a dime a dozen, but highly productive leaders are not so common. One of the easiest things for leaders to do is to bite off more than they can chew. All successful leaders are accomplished at hacking their schedule to create more time for clear thought.

Fact: Bright, talented executives with a bias to action will often take on more than they should. These leaders don't understand the value of white space. The reality is maximizing results and creating a certainty of execution is all about focus, focus, and more focus. Here's the thing—it's difficult to focus in the middle of chaos. One of the hardest things for leaders to do is to learn to create white space. The best leaders are those who understand the most productive things often happen during intentional periods of isolation used for self-reflection, introspection, and the rigor of critical thought.

See if you can think of anyone you know who resembles the following description. I recently had the chance to work with a leader who is as bright and talented as they come. That said, he had confused being busy with being productive. He was in back-to-back-to-back meetings from the time he arrived at the office until after 5:00 P.M. He didn't have any time to think much less do his own work. In fact, the working and thinking all took place after he arrived at home in the evening. This leader was working 70- hour weeks, falling behind, suffering from fatigue, and was becoming at risk.

Everyone in the company wanted a piece of this leader, but they were in effect sucking the leader dry. The leader was complicit to their own demise by not understanding the importance of maintaining adequate white space, as well as maintaining a personal life. If you're honest, more than a few people in your organization likely fit this profile—it may even be you.

While the mind of a leader may be most comfortable being oriented toward the future, he/she can only act in the here and now. The knowledge and skills required to build mastery can only be acquired when we focus on what we're currently doing. This is the definition of presence, and it is only when we operate in the present that real creativity, growth, and innovation occur.

The problem with being present is many leaders confuse this with having to do everything themselves. Have you ever interacted with someone who deals with silence by jumping in and filling the conversational void? This same thing occurs with executives who attempt to fill every open slot on the calendar with activity—this is a huge mistake.

All good leaders have matured to understand they can be fully engaged and present and yet still be alone. Smart leaders don't fill their calendars with useless activities. They strategically plan for white space allowing them to focus on highest and best use endeavors. Leading doesn't always mean doing. In fact, most often times it means pulling back and creating white space so that others can lead. This is true leadership that can be scaled.

Is your rubber band stretched so tight it's about to snap? Efficiency and productivity are not found working at or even near capacity. Rather entering the productivity zone is found working at about 60 percent to 70 percent of capacity. Operating in excess of that threshold will cause increased stress, lack of attention to detail, and errant decision making.

The old "what if I only had 'X' number of hours to work in a week, what would I focus on?" exercise is a good one. In fact, if you're reading this text, just stop right now and benchmark your activity against your reflective thoughts: Is what you're doing, in alignment with your true priorities, or have you been sucked down into the weeds?

It is important for executives to learn to apply focused leverage to a limited number of highest and best use activities rather than to continually shift gears between multiple initiatives. Resist the temptation to just advance a broad number of disparate initiatives, and alternatively focus your efforts on the completion of a few high impact objectives.

The simple reality is that if you continue to add new responsibilities to an already full plate, all of your obligations will suffer as a result. Face current challenges *head-on* by keeping your *head down* and applying focused leverage to the task at hand. Leaders who operate without margins usually hit the wall they are most desperate to avoid.

Have you noticed how some leaders are frenzied, stressed, and always playing from behind, while others are eerily clam and always appear to be a few steps ahead? It's been my experience that leaders who fall into the latter category make great use of their thought life, while those in the former category seem to forgo their alone time in lieu of being busy. Savvy leaders crave white space, whereas unseasoned leaders feel uncomfortable with open time.

One thing that can be a difficult lesson to learn is that not all engagement is necessary or productive. Leadership and engagement go hand in hand, but only when engagement happens by design rather than by default. Don't get me wrong, good things can happen with spontaneous engagement, but if you're engaging with others without intent and purpose, it likely serves as a distraction for all parties. Don't interfere with your team just because you don't understand how to use your time wisely. If you do, you'll become an annoyance known for not respecting others—this is not leadership.

I have found the best leaders are harder on themselves than anyone else could ever be. In fact, this is so much the case that the best leaders constantly self-assess and are relentless in challenging themselves. They relish their solitude because it gives them the ability to be alone with their thoughts, to challenge their logic, to refine their theories, and to test the boundaries of their intellect. It's during these quiet moments that leaders willing to be honest with themselves will examine their own flaws and frailties. They are forever in search of new ways of dealing with old problems.

The beauty of leveraging white space is it helps you avoid falling into the all too common leadership rut. It's now time to focus on hacking the status quo.

Hacking the Status Quo

Leaders who are bored, in a rut, or otherwise find themselves anesthetized by the routine have a huge problem—*they are not leading*. Leadership is a game for the mentally agile, not the brain dead. Sound harsh? It's meant to. While most of the world has succumbed to a static life imprisoned by the limitations of their own mind, real leaders are always looking beyond *what is*, thinking about the possibilities of *what if*, and acting to ensure *what's next*.

Why then do so many leaders complain about being in a rut? They get comfortable playing things safely, they rest on their laurels, they stop investing in personal growth and development, and they settle, they quit and stay—they become a leader in title only.

At one time or another we all experience the signs of boredom. Here's the thing—boredom is a state of mind. The difference between real leaders, and leaders in title only, is what they do when the creative juices begin to dwindle. Feigned leaders accept the status quo, and real leaders see the signs of boredom as the precursor to needed change.

For most people, the simple truth is excuses come easier than solutions—but who said leadership was easy? Leadership is about acclimation and reacclimation, improvising and adapting, learning and unlearning—leadership is about change.

My observations and experiences over the years have led me to a very simple conclusion: I have yet to see anyone improve their status by maintaining the status quo. If you're going to get comfortable with anything as a leader, I would suggest it be change. Change is a leader's best friend, and the one thing that will propel you forward.

Don't make excuses—make changes. Saying you don't have time for "*X*" is just code for "*X*" isn't important to me. Saying you don't have the resources needed for change is just an admission you're not very resourceful. Leadership has little to do with resources, but everything to do with resourcefulness. If you're stuck in a leadership rut, use the following five hacks to help you find your path back to real leadership:

1. **Go Break Something:** Need to reinvigorate a stale mind or a less than thriving enterprise? Try changing the corporate landscape by shifting existing roles and responsibilities, or by bringing

in fresh talent from the outside. If you want to drive innovation, lead change, and create growth, stir the pot—go break something. Slaughter a few sacred cows, challenge conventional wisdom, break a paradigm, and inject a little chaos into your static environment. Old isn't necessarily wrong, but likewise, it's not necessarily right either. Overlay a new business model on top of the existing one, and look for ways to create new advantages and make needed improvements. Reengineer a *best* practice into a *next* practice. Ask yourself this question: Is the most tenured person in a particular position, the best person for the position? If not, make a change. Don't be bored; just implement a little creative destruction.

2. **Recharge Your Brain:** A stagnant thought life is not a sign of healthy leadership. A brain is like any other energy source—it needs to be nourished in order to evolve. Whether you stimulate your brain through basic learning activities like reading, taking classes, or participating in workshops or seminars, or by just giving it some well needed rest, the important thing is to make a concerted effort in this regard. Some of my best thinking comes when I remove myself from the routine of the office and go for a run. Vacations, sabbaticals, and service projects are also quite useful for creating new thinking paradigms. I'm a big proponent of attempting to carve out new neural pathways by subjecting the brain to new and creative ways of thinking. A few of the things I'm doing this year include going cold-turkey on television (a family project), playing one game of chess each day, and studying a new language. Change-up your routine and do things differently and more productively—you'll be glad you did.

3. **Get Some Help:** Leading in isolation is dangerous. The best leaders surround themselves with wise counsel, and make a habit of seeking out sound advice. Start close to home—ask your family for their candid opinion of your shortcomings, and then listen. Those who love you the most will also give you the respect of candor. In addition to seeking guidance from your family, seek out professional advice and counsel by joining a peer group, hiring a coach, creating an advisory board, or finding a new mentor. There are abundant resources available to leaders resourceful enough to seek them out. Don't allow yourself to be held hostage by your pride, ego, arrogance, or ignorance—go get some help.

4. **Have a Vigorous Debate:** Few things kindle the creative fires like a challenging debate. By seeking out dissenting views and differing opinions, you open your mind to new ideas and perspectives. A developed mind is the result of a challenged mind. Smart leaders take their business logic and willingly subject it to brutal assault. In doing so, they often find what they believed to be close to perfect was in fact flawed. Go find the smartest people you can, and ask them to poke holes in your theories and beliefs. There is value in both validation and invalidation. Don't be afraid of being proven wrong—be afraid of thinking you're right when you're not.

5. **Fire Yourself:** In the final analysis, if you can't or won't fix yourself, or you can't or won't allow yourself to be developed by others, then it's time to pass the baton. Both you and your organization deserve more than just a leader in title, and if you cannot perform as leader, then find someone who can. Whether you transition to a co-CEO role, entrepreneur in residence, chairman of the board, consultant, take a sabbatical, or you just resign your position, all concerned parties will be better off by making a move that is likely long overdue.

Now that you're aware, refreshed, have clarity of thought, and have abandoned the status quo, it's time to get prepared.

Hacking the Preparation Gap

Do you ever find yourself in over your head? If not, I would suggest you don't spend enough time in the water. Creating white space has a dual advantage for leaders—it not only keeps them out of a rut, but it also helps them avoid getting in over their heads.

The truth is all leaders find themselves swimming in rough conditions from time to time. And trust me—it will happen to you. The difference between those who drown and those who become stronger swimmers is little more than a combination of attitude and preparation.

It was T.S. Eliot who said, "If you aren't in over your head, how do you know how tall you are?" With all due respect to Mr. Eliot, it's one thing to push past comfort zones and test your capabilities, but it's quite another thing to survive doing so. Here's the thing—good leaders take risks, but great leaders are prepared for the risks they take.

Being in over your head can lead to career-defining moments (good or bad). When leaders push personal, team, or organization boundaries one of two things is likely to happen: They'll either exceed all expectations or fall short of them. The difference between success and failure isn't found in risk taking alone, but in the planning and execution surrounding the taking of the risk. There's truth in the old military saying that "prior proper planning prevents poor performance."

I remember a time I went surfing in the frigid waters of the Pacific Northwest with my son-in-law. It was the first time I'd climbed on a surfboard in more than 30 years. I crammed myself into the wetsuit (not a pretty sight) and paddled out to the waves. The truth is, my son-in-law surfed, and I spent two hours trying not to drown. He was prepared, experienced, and in shape. He challenged himself, and I was just in over my head—literally and figuratively. He had a great time, and I just had a time of it.

My surfing experience was a great reminder that all the positive thinking in the world won't overcome certain practical realities. I don't regret surfing that day, but I do regret not being prepared for it. While I survived the experience, it was pure luck. Not everyone who takes risks without the proper preparation is so lucky. I'm not suggesting leaders shouldn't take risks, but simply that the risks be prudent ones.

The bigger issue for leaders is not the personal risk they take, but the risks they subject others to. While leaders have a responsibility to those they lead not to take unnecessary risks, they likewise have an absolute obligation to seek out and incur necessary risk. Many leaders take risks, but great leaders inculcate the planned execution of necessary risk as a cultural imperative. When calculated risk taking becomes encouraged at all levels of the enterprise it's an indicator of sound leadership and a healthy culture.

My message here is simply this: Rather than fear the rough waters, take the time and effort to prepare your team for them. Then and only then, go in search of the big waves.

Perhaps the most powerful thing about creating white space is that it presents opportunities for others to step in and raise the level of their contributions. When leaders step back and resist the temptation to do everything themselves, their organization is strengthened. When leaders become comfortable being without always doing, collaboration flourishes, and productivity is enhanced. Whether white space makes you more productive on an individual basis, or you leverage the white space to create operational depth and scale, you're better off with white space than without it.

Earlier in this chapter I encouraged leaders to go break something—to go upend the status quo. I want to share a brief story about a client, who while some may thought might have been in over his head initially, proved to be an absolute game changer as a leader.

My client had just accepted a position as President of McGraw-Hill Higher Education. He stepped into a company too comfortable with the status quo, even though the industry was in transition. An old economy industry attempting to compete in a digital era. He immediately recognized the need for change—massive, fast, and above all else, smart change.

This push for change wasn't based on an impulsive whim or youthful naiveté, but it was a calculated, courageous act of an insightful leader—he saw it as a matter of survival. He was also right.

In less than 2 years on the job, he not only transformed the company, but he also transformed the entire industry in terms of how publishing is perceived and used. He made massive changes in personnel, positioning, and made big investments into technology, actually coining the phrase "super-adaptive learning."

The leader I've been describing is Brian Kibby. The leader some initially doubted (not me) is now considered a thought leader in higher education, and is responsible for taking a storied brand from industry lagger to industry leader.

Okay, now that we've laid a good foundation, it's time to address a key leadership concept many leaders have lost sight of, trivialize, or worse yet altogether ignore—Purpose.

Chapter 2

Hacking the Purpose Gap

Great leadership cannot exist much less
flourish absent great purpose.

One of the first things I ask new a client is who do they want to be when they grow up? The next question is usually what do they stand for? These are two difficult questions to answer, but ones all great leaders can address with great clarity and specificity.

I've always said it doesn't take much talent to draw a crowd, but it requires great skill and ability to lead an engaged, passionate, and committed community of productive men and women. People can be rallied around many things, but none more powerful than purpose. All great leaders understand this premise not only with regard to their own journey, but also with regard to the organizations and teams they lead.

I want you to take a moment and examine how you identify leaders. . . . Is it by performance only, or by a broader measure? I have always believed the gold standard of leadership, the measurement of leadership greatness if you will, is based on a leader's ability to align talent and outcomes with purpose. It is at the nexus of these three areas where legends are born and history is made.

One of my favorite modern day legends in the making is Elon Musk. He is a purpose-driven leader focused on changing the world through disruptive, scalable, businesses that combine technology and energy efficiency. If you're not familiar with Elon, he used the success of his first venture (PayPal) to form three other businesses: Tesla Motors, SpaceX, and SolarCity. His latest idea, which he refers to as Hyperloop, would allow travel between major cities at the speed of sound—and all for less than the cost of a typical plane ticket.

Only in his early forties, *Forbes* ranks Musk #527 on their list of billionaires, #66 on their list of Powerful People, and #190 on the Forbes 400. What makes him so special is he's not just another inventor/entrepreneur—he's a purpose-driven leader who thinks far beyond his self-interest. He has the ability to rally people around their belief in his ability to transform vision into reality. Listen to Elon talk about what he does, and you'll rarely hear the words "I" or "me" as he is clearly focused on a larger purpose—improving the lives of others.

Similarly to Elon Musk, any nation, army, business enterprise (for profit or not), or political or social cause, it's the purpose-driven leaders who stand apart. They are able to rally people around something bigger, bolder, and more impactful than themselves. It is these purpose-driven leaders who have learned to hack into the hearts and minds of those they lead.

Even a brief review of some of history's great military leaders demonstrates the power of purpose. Think about it like this, how many of those you lead would willingly risk their lives for your cause? Even a cursory examination of military leaders like William the Conqueror, Cyrus the Great, Ulysses S. Grant, Robert E. Lee, Georgy Zhukov, George Marshall, Douglas MacArthur, and Norman Schwarzkopf will reveal each were fueled by a clear sense of purpose. Whether or not you agree with their purpose is not the issue; the fact they were able to use purpose to leave legacies that survived long past their command is what I want you to think about.

Think for a moment of the great reformers. . . . If not for an unyielding conviction to a greater purpose by the likes of Martin

Luther, John Calvin, William Wilberforce, Abraham Lincoln, Frederick Douglass, Susan B. Anthony, Martin Luther King, Nelson Mandela, Aung San Suu Kyi, and so on, the world might today be lacking many of our personal and religious freedoms.

If not for the strength of purpose that propelled the founders and framers to give birth to a nation, the United States of America might not exist. This great experiment in democracy required 56 purpose-driven men like George Washington, John Adams, Thomas Jefferson, Benjamin Rush, Benjamin Franklin, and others, to subordinate personal arguments and beliefs to a higher purpose. Following is an excerpt from the Declaration of Independence:

> When in the Course of human events, it becomes necessary for one people to dissolve the political bands which have connected them with another, and to assume among the powers of the earth, the separate and equal station to which the Laws of Nature and of Nature's God entitle them, a decent respect to the opinions of mankind requires that they should declare the causes which impel them to the separation.
>
> We hold these truths to be self-evident, that all men are created equal, that they are endowed by their Creator with certain unalienable Rights, that among these are Life, Liberty and the pursuit of Happiness.—That to secure these rights, Governments are instituted among Men, deriving their just powers from the consent of the governed,—That whenever any Form of Government becomes destructive of these ends, it is the Right of the People to alter or to abolish it, and to institute new Government, laying its foundation on such principles and organizing its powers in such form, as to them shall seem most likely to effect their Safety and Happiness.

Are you beginning to see the power of purpose? If you believe my premise that purpose-driven leaders have fueled the greatest accomplishments in world history, then why would anyone believe for a moment that a business should operate apart from or without purpose? The reality is that many organizations in today's world have devolved to the point where there is no clear purpose, and therefore, there is exists no real leadership.

Following in the Footsteps of Greatness—The Movement Hack

The secret sauce to purpose is found in a leader's ability to scale personal and professional purpose into a cause embraced and evangelized by others. Just as with the historical examples previously cited, every so often a time arrives where society reaches a crossroads—where the situation and/or circumstances so obviously demand change that a populist mandate—a *movement* takes place.

I would submit we find ourselves at just such a crossroads today. We are in a crisis of leadership, and our world is suffering greatly at the hands of people who confuse their desire for an ego boost, their quest for power, and their thirst for greed with leadership. It's time to say enough is enough—it's time for a leadership movement.

Movements are nothing new. Some movements have been evolutionary, while others have been revolutionary. Some have been misguided or misunderstood and have been short-lived, while others have taken deep root and changed the world for better. I'm afraid we've reached a place in history where if we don't draw a line in the sand and say we will no longer tolerate personal exploits as a poor excuse for leadership we may be too late.

It's time for a *leadership movement* that values engagement, open dialogue, and candid discourse above personal gain. A movement is a cause greater than one's self—it's a populist groundswell rather than an elitist academic exercise. A movement is intentional, impassioned, and biased toward action. A movement requires a vision that's inclusive, collaborative, and has an orientation toward service. Most of all, a movement requires people committed to change. These things can only be accomplished if fueled by a shared purpose.

This book is meant to be an encouragement for you to start making personal and professional changes. It's time to dispense with the trivial, and begin majoring in the majors. We must bring the best leadership minds together—I'm not talking about like-minded thinkers, but big thinkers—deep thinkers. Those open to challenging what is considered "normal" with the goal of shattering outdated thinking.

We must dialog and debate, but most of all, we must listen, learn and act. We must focus on what's wrong with leadership and fix it.

I'd ask you to become a better leader and awaken those around you to the dire need we have for a movement of leadership.

So, what's your cause—your greater purpose—your opportunity to create a movement? Pursue these things. Rally people around this new-found shared purpose, and go change the world. Not everyone can be the next Elon Musk, but anyone can make a difference.

Purpose is so critical to successful leadership that entire books have been written on the topic. In fact, one of my favorites is *Lead with Purpose* (AMACOM, 2011) by John Baldoni. John chairs our leadership development practice at N2growth, and is the consummate purpose-driven leader. His purpose is clear—to help develop better leaders. This purpose guides his writing, teaching, speaking, and coaching. It gives him great passion, clarity of thought, a framework for making decisions, and helps him pursue the right opportunities. This is purpose-driven leadership.

Even though there are many great works published on purpose, I cannot imagine trying to address leadership without devoting at least one entire chapter to the topic. Purpose is the foundational cornerstone for great leadership. It's what makes the difference between failure and success. Likewise, it must be understood when purpose is viewed as little more than an afterthought, individuals, teams, and organizations place themselves at the risk of serving two very dangerous masters—ego and greed.

The text that follows is my short manifesto on purpose. I'll break it down into two categories: personal and organizational purpose.

Individual Purpose—Hacking the Purpose Continuum

Individual purpose is found by connecting key points across what I refer to as *The Purpose Continuum* (see Figure 2.1).

The Purpose Continuum (TPC) is designed to illustrate that in order for leaders to maximize the three areas on the far right of the

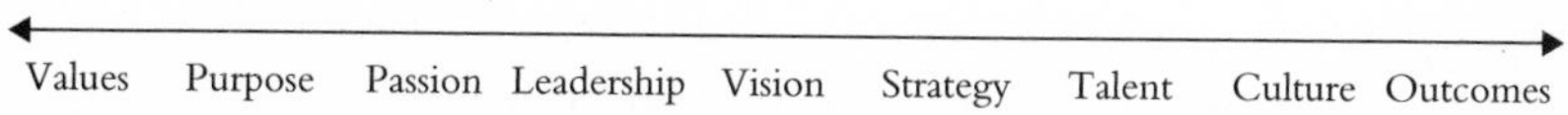

Values   Purpose   Passion   Leadership   Vision   Strategy   Talent   Culture   Outcomes

Figure 2.1 The Purpose Continuum

spectrum, they must first align and integrate all of areas that precede them on the left of the continuum.

A business process framework I created more than 20 years ago underpins the basis of TPC. Much like an algebraic formula, there is a correct order of operation for leadership as well. Even though the following sequence is more than two decades old, it's as relevant today as it was then:

> **Values** should underpin **Vision**, which dictates **Mission**, which determines **Strategy**, which surfaces **Goals** that frame **Objectives**, which in turn drives the **Tactics** that tell an organization what **Resources**, **Infrastructure** and **Processes** are needed to support a certainty of execution.
>
> **—Mike Myatt**

The best leaders understand the critical importance of transforming personal values into a greater sense of purpose. It is only at the point where leaders become committed to purpose that they're able to surrender it, and let purpose guide their approach to leadership. It's often this revelation that transforms leaders in title only into passionate purpose-driven leaders.

Leadership means many things to many people. And not all forms of leadership are created equal. Leadership can represent a pursuit, discipline, practice, passion, skill, competency, obligation, or duty. Leadership driven by any of these constructs can be effective, but where leadership really gets interesting is when it combines all of these traits to become purpose-driven. Show me a leader without purpose, and I'll show you a leader destined to fall short of their potential.

If you're chasing a position and not a higher purpose, you may want to rethink your approach. If you value self-interest above service beyond self, you simply don't understand the concept of leadership. Real leadership means you care first and foremost about something beyond yourself. It means your focus is on leading others to a better place—even if it means you take a back seat, or end up with no seat at all. Power often comes with leadership, but it's not what drives real leaders. The best leaders are driven by purpose.

I need to pause here for a moment and draw an important distinction; there exists a gap between success and significance—that gap is purpose. Leaders can achieve success without having purpose, but they'll find it extremely difficult to achieve significance. Purpose leverages success into significance. This is far more than a debate on semantics.

My hope in calling out this distinction is to have you adjust your thinking when it comes to the definition of success. My clients tend to be very successful individuals prior to finding me. My goal is to simply help them leverage their success into becoming more significant leaders over the course of our dealings. The reality is that far too many people either confuse success with significance, or they are so focused on success that they are actually blind to the meaning of significance. The simple truth of the matter is with the proper focus you can have your cake and eat it, too.

Take a look around, and you'll see most people use their knowledge, resources, and experience to acquire things in an attempt to satisfy their personal desires, which in their minds constitute success. Contrast this with the leaders who use their knowledge, resources, and experience to serve and benefit others, which by my standards constitutes significance. Just as success must be defined before it can be achieved, so must significance. While both require sacrifice, success comes at a great price and is often based upon the compromise of values. Significance, on the other hand, is purpose-driven by personal values and is a gift that cannot be purchased.

See if this example resonates with you. Contrast a politician (often successful and rarely significant) with a statesman (usually both). It has been said a politician is concerned with winning the election and a statesman is concerned about future generations. The politician makes promises and is motivated by pride, ego, notoriety, and personal success. The statesman keeps commitments, is motivated by service above and beyond self, and by making a lasting difference.

Typical politicians spew tired rhetoric while lining their pockets, and have little hope of becoming significant. The true statesman is a breath of fresh air whose only pursuit is to make a positive difference in the lives of others. The politician in pursuit of his goal will live in infamy or insignificance. By contrast, the statesman in pursuit of the best interests of others will become both successful and significant.

Sure, for those "who get it" success and significance are one and the same, but for most professionals success begins and ends with the achievement of a certain list of personal goals with little regard to the impact on others. These people confuse success with significance, and regardless of their wealth and professional accomplishments, they won't accomplish the true greatness that only comes through making significant contributions to something other than one's self. I don't care how your resume reads, what your net worth is, or what your W-2 shows . . . what I care about is your motivation, and what you do with what you have.

You'll find it difficult to think of any great leader, or any great organization, where purpose was misunderstood or lacking. Purpose is what the best employees are seeking when looking for an organization to work for. Those same talented employees are looking for their leaders to have a clear sense of purpose guiding their thinking and their actions. A shared purpose is what fuels leaders, attracts talent, and creates a sustainable culture of leadership. A unified purpose can endure all things.

Purpose is one of the few things all great leaders have in common. Great leaders have a clearly defined purpose, while average leaders just show up for work. Purpose fuels passion, which creates focus and, in turn fuels high performance. It is these characteristics that afford great leaders a competitive advantage over those who don't understand the dynamics of this linkage.

To put it bluntly, leading without purpose is nothing short of an exercise in frivolity. If you want to understand purpose, begin by learning the power of pursuit.

Hacking the Pursuit Gap

One of the most often overlooked aspects of leadership is the need for pursuit. Know this—you will find it difficult, if not impossible to recognize your personal, professional, or organizational purpose unless you pursue it.

At its essence, *leadership is pursuit*—pursuit of excellence, of elegance, of truth, of what's next, of what if, of change, of value, of results, of relationships, of service, of knowledge, and of something bigger than yourself—pursuit of purpose.

Here's the thing—pursuit leads to attainment. What you pursue will determine the paths you travel, the people you associate with, the character you develop, and, ultimately, what you do or don't achieve. Having a mind-set focused on pursuit is so critical to leadership that lacking this one quality can sentence you to mediocrity or even obsolescence. The manner, method, and motivation behind any pursuit are what set truly great leaders apart from the masses. If you want to become a great leader, become a great pursuer.

A failure to embrace pursuit is to cede opportunity to others. Think about pursuit in these terms:

- A leader's failure to pursue clarity leaves them amidst the fog.
- Their failure to pursue creativity relegates them to the routine and mundane.
- Their failure to pursue talent sentences them to a world of isolation.
- Their failure to pursue change approves apathy.
- Their failure to pursue wisdom and discernment subjects them to distraction and folly.
- Their failure to pursue character leaves a question mark on their integrity.
- Their failure to pursue purpose will keep them from their destiny.

Let me put this as simply as I can—you cannot attain what you do not pursue.

Smart leaders understand it's not just enough to pursue, but pursuit must be intentional, focused, consistent, aggressive, and unyielding— it must have purpose. You must pursue the right things, for the right reasons, and at the right times. Perhaps most of all, the best forms of pursuit enlist others in the chase. Pursuit in its purest form is highly collaborative, very inclusive, and easily transferable. Pursuit operates at greatest strength when it leverages velocity and scale.

I also want to caution you against trivial pursuits—don't confuse pursuit with simple goal setting. Outcomes are clearly important, but as a leader, it's what happens after the outcome that you need to pursue. Pursue discovery, seek dissenting opinions, develop your ability, unlearn by embracing how much you don't know, and find the kind of vision that truly does see around corners. Don't use your pursuits to shift paradigms, pursue breaking them. Knowing what not to pursue is just as important as knowing what to pursue.

It's important to keep in mind that nothing tells the world more about leaders than what or whom they pursue, or why they pursue it. That which you pursue *is* that which you value. If your message to your organization is that you value talent, but you don't treat people well and don't spend time developing said talent, then I would suggest you value rhetoric more than talent. Put simply, you can wax eloquent all you like, but your actions will ultimately reveal what you truly value.

Lastly, the best leaders pursue being better leaders. They know that to fail in this pursuit is nothing short of a guarantee they'll be replaced by those who succeed. All leaders would be well served to go back to school on what I refer to as the art and science of *pursuitology*.

As you pursue and eventually discover your purpose, you'll also discover a newfound sense of passion. While passion can be a great catalyst, it can also lead you astray—knowing how to hack passion is essential to productive, purposed leadership.

Hacking the Passion Gap

Because purpose creates passion, you'll be hard pressed to find any great leader who does not also possess great passion. That said, while passion is often talked about, it's not well understood. The word "passion" comes from the Latin root, which quite literally means, "to suffer." Therefore it should come as no surprise that those who are passionate in their pursuits are often willing to make personal and professional sacrifices in order to reach their objectives that the unimpassioned simply won't make—they have purpose.

You'll find no argument from me that passion can almost single-handedly propel leaders to new heights of success. History is littered with accounts of marginally talented individuals who have risen to greatness based upon little more than being passionate about the pursuit of their objective. Passion creates a *refuse to lose* mentality, which can enable the average person to move outside comfort zones, take on greater risk, go the extra mile, and achieve phenomenal results.

However it's important to note the same trait capable of propelling you to the top can also send you over the edge. Passion is not aptitude, nor is it competency, and neither is it totally unique. The only difference between irrational exuberance, folly, or impulsivity and passion is clear sense of purpose. These are nuances lost on many.

You see, passion without perspective and/or reason can actually serve to distort one's perception of reality. These distorted perceptions can quickly place a leader on a very slippery slope blurring the lines between fact and fiction—very dangerous territory for any leader. Have you ever known people who wanted something to be true so badly that they started to adopt positions and manufacture circumstances to support their own false reality? Just because you can convince yourself (or others) that your position is correct, doesn't necessarily mean that it is.

Just as there exists a very fine line between brilliance and insanity, there also exists a fine line between passion and many negative traits such as narrow-mindedness, narcissism, fanaticism, delusion, and even paranoia. For instance, there is a big difference between leaders who are passionate about their business and ones who are emotionally overinvested in their business. Passion balanced by perspective and reason can reveal purpose, but passion absent those filters can just as easily impede purpose. Believing your own smoke is often different than being grounded in reality.

Healthy passion for one's business actually brings focus and clarity of thought, which serve to accelerate growth and create sustainable success. However, being emotionally overinvested in one's business can lead to irrational decisioning, prideful or ego-driven actions, the use of flawed business logic, and poor execution. These are the regrettable and completely avoidable precursors to unnecessary loss and/or failure.

It is not at all uncommon for entrepreneurs and executives to be too close to the forest to see the trees. Passionate professionals thinking clearly will seek independent counsel and advice to continually gut-check and refine their thinking. Emotionally overinvested professionals will either avoid counsel or surround themselves with legions of *yes-men*.

Effective leadership teams have a balance of left-brain and right-brain thinkers that come from a variety of backgrounds in order to draw from the broadest possible array of experiences when formulating positions and options. Emotionally overinvested professionals tend to surround themselves with very small teams of like-minded individuals from similar backgrounds who tend to reinforce each others' thinking instead of challenging it.

Finding Organizational Purpose
Begins with Hacking Why

Attempting to define organizational purpose without asking and answering *why* is like trying to start your engine without placing the key in the ignition—it just won't work.

One of my favorite books in recent years has been Simon Sinek's *Start with Why* (Penguin, 2009). While the book is a fast, simple read, it focuses on all the right issues. Moreover, Simon cites both historical and current references supporting his belief as to the relevance of formulating purpose by starting with why. Simon and I agree on this point.

I have always said, smart leaders focus on the *why*, align the *who* with the *why*, and then allow the *who* to determine the appropriate course of action with regard to *what* and *how*—say that fast five times. All kidding aside, read this last statement a few times and let it sink in.

Don't be in the business of business—be in the business of leadership. At its core, leadership is the business of defining and articulating vision (*why*), and then aligning people (*who*) with said vision—these are the two key strategic elements of leadership (leadership + purpose + people = culture). The tactical elements of leadership (*what* and *how*) are best accomplished only after the *why* is clearly understood, and the *who* is soundly in place. A business that pursues a purpose-driven culture of leadership will simply outperform a business that focuses solely on profit.

Many organizations attract people with compensation—the great organizations attract people with a clearly articulated and compelling purpose. Examine the most successful brands in the market, and you'll find shared values and a common purpose—they possess a clear understanding of why. Look at any of the *it* companies—if you wonder what makes them different, wonder no more. They all understand why they exist. They understand their purpose.

Hacking the Profit Gap

In recent decades when people thought of purpose-driven organizations their minds would naturally gravitate toward the nonprofits. Lofty ideals and thoughts of making the world a better place were items of interest in social or academic endeavors, but business was all about profit. The funny thing is, times have changed and it's catching many for-profit businesses by surprise.

Many organizations talk about a higher purpose—it's listed on their website, in their vision statement, and from time to time they'll even check the CSR (community social responsibility) box. Sadly, these steps are a far cry from seamlessly integrating a higher purpose into their strategy and day-to-day operations.

Let's conduct a brief test—I challenge you to name 10 for-profit businesses whose higher purpose is the foundation for their culture, the basis for their talent management platform, the underpinning for their business model, and the core of their brand promise. I've asked countless executives to take this test and by the time they get to the fifth or sixth company they're beginning to really stretch the intellectual honesty of the exercise.

At companies like Method, Kashi, Southwest Airlines, Zappos, Costco, Patagonia, and Whole Foods, employees know why they go to work each day, and it's not just for a paycheck. They show up for work each day to be part of something with a bigger purpose. Make no mistake—purpose is the ultimate competitive advantage.

The reality is that most businesses and many leaders suffer from having a purpose gap—the bigger picture is simply missing from the leadership equation in many organizations. There's far too much emphasis on short-term financial metrics and not nearly enough emphasis on *doing well by doing good*.

What many leaders fail to understand is that purpose drives profit, but rarely does profit create purpose. Moreover, purpose can drive profit and align interests with more cohesion, velocity, and scale than any other alternative substitute.

The interesting thing about purpose is that while it may be elusive, it's never too late to discover it or to redefine it. Let me offer an example. I've had the pleasure of working closely with a Fortune 100 health care company going through a CEO succession over the past two years. The outgoing CEO was extremely successful with his vision, and as a result, the company was among the most highly regarded in the industry. However, the incoming chief executive was stepping into an industry in transition.

With questions looming about the impact of the Affordable Care Act, the systems stress of a rapidly aging population, the complexity of coordinating services over a continuum of care, the uncertainty of government reimbursements, an ever-changing public policy landscape, and a whole host of other issues, it was clear to the successor CEO that changes would need to be made to the business model, the culture, and the brand.

He recognized the need to align stakeholders around a clearly defined set of values and a purpose that would guide his organization through the rough waters ahead. Countless hours were spent on definition, creation, and refinement of the things that matter. It was of little consequence to the incoming CEO how successful the company was in the past, his focus was on what needed to be done to secure the best outcome for its members and associates going forward.

Values were defined, vision was recast, strategy was refreshed, and the organizational purpose was clear. These changes attracted new talent, reinvigorated existing talent, improved the culture, and focused the business. Those of us involved in the process were watching an aircraft carrier begin to turn on a dime under the leadership of a focused, passionate, purpose-driven chief executive.

Here's the thing—nothing was broken at this organization. In fact, many observers both inside and outside the company would have said it was *best in class*. It takes great courage to bring change to an organization at the top of its game. The leadership lesson here was that in less than two short years best became even better. When leaders align values, vision, culture, and talent they create purpose. The company's name is Humana and the CEO is Bruce Broussard.

What Bruce intuitively understood, which many CEOs do not, is that the only way to truly maintain advantage is by continuing to create it. How many once category dominant companies have fallen from the top of their game because they chose to play defense rather than to play offense by continuing to innovate? Too many—the following list contains just a few examples of companies that have either declared bankruptcy, been broken-up, spun, sold, or have just fallen into mediocrity:

- American Motors Corp.
- Arthur Andersen

- Beatrice
- Blockbuster
- Borders
- CompUSA
- Dell
- DeLorean
- E.F. Hutton
- Enron
- G.I. Joe's
- General Foods
- Hollywood Video
- Kodak
- Lehman Brothers
- Lionel
- MCI WorldCom
- Montgomery Ward
- Motorola
- Nortel
- Oldsmobile
- Pan Am
- Schwinn
- Standard Oil
- TWA
- Woolworth's

Again, these companies did not fail as much as their leadership failed to lead. Great leaders know that to protect what they have they must build on it. These leaders lost touch with their purpose, their vision, and their passion.

Let me conclude my discussion on purpose by describing what it's not—profit. To the chagrin of many, profit isn't the reason a business exits; it's a by-product of a purpose-driven business. Those in a position of leadership motivated solely by profit agenda may be referred to as many things, but the term *leader* should not be among them. While I noted this before, it bears repeating: A lesson lost on many is profit doesn't drive purpose, but purpose certainly drives profit—great leaders understand this; average leaders do not.

Don't get me wrong, I'm not opposed to leaders who profit, or businesses that make a profit. That said, leaders driven only by profit will find that while they may be successful for a season, they'll eventually come to realize a pure profit agenda is not sustainable. Great leaders make the transition from profit to purpose and are handsomely rewarded for doing so.

When purpose is disconnected from profit, decisions gaps and blind spots become the rule and not the exception. However when leaders awaken to the fact that purpose and profit are not mutually exclusive interests, but mutually synergistic catalysts, wonderful opportunities for hacking the purpose gap become plentiful.

Perhaps the greatest benefit to a clearly defined purpose is it helps frame a road map from the present to the future. In the next chapter I'll address the most common misperceptions about what lies ahead, and how to hack your way to a better future.

Chapter 3

Hacking the Future Gap

Great leaders don't move toward the future, they bring the future to them—they pull the future forward.

In Chapter 2 I provided you with several examples of companies that at one point had very bright futures only to let them slip away. The leadership of those organizations simply didn't understand how to navigate from the present to the future. I decided to begin this chapter by examining a case study of two different retailers and how their view of the future is shaping the destiny of their respective organizations.

This is one of my favorite case studies—it's a David and Goliath story of sorts. What I most enjoy about this case study is that the story is still being written. In other words, it isn't over yet. The other thing I like about this example is there isn't a winner or loser. Both companies are highly successful using different approaches. It serves to illustrate that it's not the business model that matters, but the commitment of leadership to pursue a clearly articulated, and well-aligned vision for the future. The following case study compares the world's largest retailer (Walmart) with Wegmans, a family-owned regional supermarket chain.

You're likely familiar with the story of my Goliath—at the time of this writing, Walmart employs more than 2 million associates in more than 27 countries with fiscal year 2013 revenues of more than $460 billion dollars. Almost 250 million consumers visit their stores on a weekly basis. The size and scale of Walmart is nothing short of mind-boggling.

You may not be as familiar with my David (unless you live in one of their market areas)—Wegmans does more than $6 billion in annual revenue, and employs more than 40,000 people across its more than 80 stores in New York, Pennsylvania, New Jersey, Virginia, Maryland, and Massachusetts. As mind-numbing as Walmart's size is, so are the ratings of both employee and customer satisfaction at Wegmans.

Let's begin the examination by looking at what each organization believes. The following statement is listed on Wegmans website as "What We Believe":

At Wegmans, we believe that good people, working toward a common goal, can accomplish anything they set out to do.

In this spirit, we set our goal to be the very best at serving the needs of our customers. Every action we take should be made with this in mind.

We also believe that we can achieve our goal only if we fulfill the needs of our own people. To our customers and our people we pledge continuous improvement, and we make the commitment

Every Day You Get Our Best

The following statements reflect two versions of the Walmart mission statement, and I've also included a statement of further clarification by the company's founder, the late Sam Walton:

Walmart Mission Statement:

"We save people money so they can live better." Or "Save Money. Live Better."

Walton's Clarification:

If we work together, we'll lower the cost of living for everyone . . . we'll give the world an opportunity to see what it's
like to save and have a better life.

The reality is both companies are great organizations very successful in their own right. They just define success differently. Both are
highly philanthropic, and their giving far exceeds that of most of their
peers. But it's their purpose as reflected in the respective statements
above that drives them.

There is no better company on the face of the planet at supply chain
management and driving down costs than Walmart. Likewise there is no
better company when it comes to treating the employees and customers
well than Wegmans. Walmart defines success by doing "low cost" better than
anyone, and Wegmans defines success by doing "service" better than anyone.

Both models work, both are sustainable, both attract good talent,
both attract loyal consumers, and both are driven by a purpose-aligned
vision for the future. You can pick companies in any sector that exhibit
these traits. It's the organizations that fail in these areas that fall off the
radar screen into mediocrity, obscurity, and irrelevance. Walmart and
Wegmans see their future clearly—do you?

How to See around Corners—Hacking
the Vision Gap

Here's the thing—life is just plain easier when you can see what's ahead
of you. Some leaders clearly have poor vision—their most polished
skill seems to be running into brick walls. Other leaders simply possess
adequate vision—they avoid the obvious speed bumps, but fail to stand
out from the crowd. Then there are those leaders who possess legend-
ary vision—the rare few who can see around corners. What you may not
realize is that *everyone* can learn to see around corners, and it's not as hard
as you think—if you understand how to hack the future gap, that is.

To better illustrate the value of hacking leadership, I'll use the anal-
ogy of a magician's trick. A magic show is not real magic, but merely
an elaborate illusion. Magicians simply know something you don't—

how the trick works. This premise holds true with visionary business leaders as well—they've learned the tricks of their trade (the hacks) that others have yet to master. Great leaders can connect dots that seem disconnected to others. Let me be clear; good leadership isn't a form of hocus-pocus, it's simply something to be learned. My question is this: Will you do what it takes to learn your craft?

My goal for this chapter is to provide you with a different perspective on the future. I not only want you to change how you view the future, but I want you to understand you can change the future in ways you might not realize. Your leadership can either shape a very bright future, or your lack of leadership can eviscerate the potential for a bright future—you have a choice.

I want to start by sharing my thoughts on how we should define the future. You see, there's a misconception about the future—that it's some distant, ethereal, far-off event. It's not . . . it happens in just a fraction of a second. And what's particularly interesting is the future is constantly refreshing itself—second after second, after second. As long as you're still vertical and breathing the future is going to happen—the question is what are you going to do about it?

Are you going to bring a purposed design element to the future, or are you just going to let it unfold? I want you to view the future as your playground—something that can be hacked—something you can influence with your thinking and your actions.

To Hack the Future You Must Have Clear Perspective on the Past

When I think of someone who possessed a clear understanding of the path to the future, I think of the individual who envisioned placing a man on the moon. It was President John F. Kennedy, who said:

> For time and the world do not stand still. Change is the law of life. And those who look only to the past or the present are certain to miss the future.

What President Kennedy knew more than five decades ago, and Michelangelo knew several centuries ago, is that innovation, growth, and development cannot occur by pretending we live in a world that has long since passed us by. All great leaders are forward thinking and leaning. Leading in the twenty-first century affords no safe haven for eighteenth-, nineteenth-, and twentieth-century thinkers.

The reality is that old, static, and/or institutionalized thinking will gate the pace of forward progress faster than just about anything. If you want to expose yourself as an out-of-touch, dated leader, keep trying to address today's issues and opportunities with yesterday's thinking.

Let's get right to it—history is useful for many things, but the experience and wisdom acquired from days gone by should be a springboard to the future, not an excuse for living in the past. Smart leaders simply don't waste precious resources on refining initiatives—they invest in reimagination efforts. Leaders would be well served to apply reimagination to all aspects of their business, but particularly with regard to constantly reimagining how they lead.

Examine any study on the rate of change, and you'll find we're living in an unprecedented time. The rate of change is clearly outpacing most leaders' ability to learn and unlearn. Many leaders struggle to remain current, much less find a way to move ahead of the curve. Here's the thing—if leaders are stuck in the past, their organizations will be forced to travel a very rough road to the future.

To Hack the Future You Must Understand How to Navigate the Present

Smart leaders don't allow themselves or those they lead to get bogged down in the present at the expense of the future. The best leaders understand the present is nothing more than a platform for the envisioning of, and positioning for, the future. Leaders must become comfortable living in the present while being able to keep an eye on the future. It's not an *either/or* thing—it's an *and* thing.

While it's important for leaders to balance their present responsibilities with their future obligations, they must not let the former overshadow the latter. I want you to rethink your perspective on the present vs. the future by examining the contrasts I've laid out in Table 3.1.

Table 3.1 The Present versus the Future

The Present	The Future
Where battles are fought	Where wars are won
Where values are stated	Where values become culture
Where potential is recognized	Where potential is realized
Where need for change is identified	Where innovation becomes reality
Where pursuit takes place	Where purpose is fulfilled
Where planning occurs	Where outcomes are achieved
Where leaders are developed	Where leadership becomes ubiquitous
Where success is made	Where significance is judged

It must be understood by all leaders that the present is the transformative battleground for the future. Your actions in the present will determine what type of future you and your organization will have. If you do not "win" the present you will have no ability to "win" the future.

That said, too much focus on the present without regard for its impact on the future will only create a larger gap between the two. Focus only on the aspects of the present that lead you toward the future. The big take-away here should be your recognition that the gap between the present and the future is only as large or small as the quality, commitment and character of your leadership. A win in one realm without a corresponding win in the other will produce nothing more than a pyrrhic victory.

Hacking the New Normal

There's no shortage of recent commentary on how the "new normal" is impacting business. Here's the thing—most of it flat misses the mark. It doesn't take a great deal of insightfulness to recognize businesses are navigating new levels of technical complexity, economic uncertainty, political acrimony, and consumer cautiousness. That said, the new normal isn't to be feared; it should be embraced. Those leaders derailed by economic challenges simply failed to successfully hack their way through the storm.

The best leaders aren't seeking a safe harbor in the ordinary. They're seeking to navigate past the status quo into the realm of the extraordinary. Smart leaders recognize economic slow-downs are not all doom and gloom. In fact, the smartest executives understand that swimming upstream against the conventional wisdom of the risk-averse can actually create significant opportunities for growth. This is the lens smart leaders use to view the new normal.

Business leaders who blame the economy for poor business performance are simply redirecting blame for their bad leadership on a target of convenience. If an economic downturn ruins a business, then it wasn't much of a business to begin with. Severe business downturns or failures are a result of poor leadership—not economic conditions. A bad economy doesn't cause good leadership to become bad, it simply reveals poor leadership that is no longer able to hide behind frothy market conditions, which so conveniently masked their shortcomings.

There are hundreds of studies that show businesses that focus on growth during bad economic times do better than competitors who lose their focus and attempt to wait it out on the sidelines. Leadership is not a spectator sport—it doesn't lend itself well to a passive, or worse yet, regressive posture. Don't fall prey to trying to do more with less, develop the ability to secure the talent and resources needed to create a strategic advantage. Using a lack of resources as an excuse is just an indicator that you're not very resourceful.

Great leaders not only embrace the new normal, they look to constantly recreate the next version of it. Succumbing to comfort zones and status quo thinking simply creates barriers to innovation and change. The new normal affords leaders the opportunity to reexamine everything, abandon outdated thinking, and challenge dominant logic. By perpetually creating the next new normal, your business can remain in a constant state of reinvention.

This book is my plea for you to consider breaking the existing leadership paradigms within your organization. Not that you need it, but you have my permission to find a few sacred cows and lead them to slaughter. Examine what you measure and why you measure it. Look at how decisions are made and who is allowed to make them. Inject youth where none presently exists. Replace the office squatters (those who have mentally quit, but failed to physically leave). Stop rewarding static thinking by embracing dissenting opinion and diversity of thought.

Use your creativity and leadership ability to leverage the next version of the new normal to be disruptive, create competitive advantage where none previously existed, acquire better talent, become more engaged and collaborative, and rebuff apathy and mediocrity at every level.

What's the next new normal look like for your organization? I would suggest you create the new normal by design. This is best accomplished by learning to pull the future forward.

Great Leaders Hack the Future by Pulling It Forward

I opened this chapter with a quote about pulling the future forward, but now I want to explain exactly what I mean. I have long observed most people plot a very complex path to the future. Year by year, month by month, day by day, task by task, and event by event, most leaders hope to have the attainment of a goal intersect with a pre-destined point in time. While there's nothing particularly wrong with this process, it has one distinct disadvantage—the focus point for most people is set too far out. They are focused on chasing a point in time rather than drawing that point in time closer to them.

Conventional wisdom dictates that you move to the future, but the most successful leaders don't move toward the future, they bring the future to them—they pull the future forward. They focus on disrupting things *now*—not at some point in the future. They apply their creativity, not to a distant event, but to the immediate opportunity in which they can accelerate the future.

If you want to lead more effectively, shorten the distance between the future and present. Inspiring innovation and leading change call for more than process—they require the adoption of a cultural mind-set. Leaders who protect the status quo through control must surrender to change in order to secure the future for their organization.

Don't be the leader who rewards herd mentality, and me-too thinking. Don't be the leader who encourages people not to fail or not to take risks. Be the leader who both models and gives permission to do the exact opposite of the aforementioned—be a leader who leads.

If you take nothing else from this section I hope you don't miss the power of this statement: *The best view of the future is found through the lens of the people.* To understand the future, one must truly, deeply, and richly understand people. People are the key to the future. It's the people who make today's decisions (good and bad) that pave the path into the future. If you want to predict the future, you must become very good at understanding and engaging people of influence. Sure, go ahead and study business, but if you don't master the study of people, all the business knowledge in the world won't help. Following are three hacks to help you better understand the people.

1. **The Motivation Hack**

   You'll never understand people until you know what motivates them. To predict the future, you must be able to reasonably predict the actions of people, so you must understand their motivations. Motivation often tells the tale of a person's credibility, influence, and effectiveness. One of the first things I like to understand when working with leaders is *what drives them*. Their motivations speak to who they are, what they value, how they work, and why they do what they do.

2. **Hacking the Rhetoric**

   There's a reason for the old axiom "talk is cheap"—it's true. More important than what people *say* is what they *do*. If you really want to understand what leaders believe at their core, observe the decisions they make (or don't make), the relationships they value (or don't value), the courage they display (or fail to display), and the challenges they accept (or walk away from). To listen is good, to watch is important, but to understand is essential. There is no reason to be surprised by people's behavior, unless you've failed to observe it.

3. **The Observation Hack**

   Few things will help gain insight into the future of a career, project, product, or company like taking a close look into the character and commitment of the people driving them. Look into any leadership failure, and upon even the most cursory examination, you'll find indications of failure were everywhere well in advance of the event itself. The signs of success and failure are always clearly visible to those who look. Visionary leaders see the reality of a situation, event, or circumstance. They refrain from the common delusion of seeing what they choose to see, and they base their actions/

decisions on a realistic interpretation of the signs. The only way you should ever be surprised by someone's character is if you have failed to recognize it for what it is.

Hacking Generational Complexity

No rational discussion about the future can be held without talking about cross-generational leadership. Leaders' biggest struggle is not the routine of the familiar, but the journey of the unknown. It's getting from where they are to where they want to be strategically, tactically, organizationally, developmentally, and, most importantly, relationally that matters. It's been said that the best way to impact your future is to change your present circumstances. And quite frankly, I can't think of a better place to ignite that change than by helping you to gain a better understanding of how to connect with what *IS* the future—the younger generation—the next generation of leaders.

Let me be as clear as I can—there are still far too many leaders who believe in having someone *earn their stripes* and *pay their dues*—please don't do this, don't be this person. It's not productive—*it doesn't work.* Don't focus on restricting development, Focus on unlocking passion and potential. Don't seek to be affirmed by the tenured—seek to be challenged by those who offer something new. Don't cater to the past, but focus on the future. I'm going to encourage you to draw a line in the sand and ask you to absolutely refuse to allow your organization to reek of the stale scent of status quo.

I'm going to ask you to stop complaining about the younger generation, and instead become very intentional and very fluent in your understanding of them. By all means, mentor and develop them, but it's time to make a paradigm shift in traditional thinking and for leaders to check their egos. Learning is not solely a top-down initiative. What I want you to understand is that the next generation has just as much to offer you, and just as much to teach you.

Here's the thing; cross-generational corporate experiments aren't working too well. Put another way, most leaders haven't figured out how to deal with the challenges of integrating different generations and their respective belief systems. We're all experiencing the same collision of generations within the workforce, and while some are reaping the benefits of turning friction into opportunity, most are not. This is because many leaders have generations competing with one another rather than learning from each other.

Let's take a closer look at these generations—Boomers (those born between 1946 and 1964) represent a huge segment of our population, and the Millennials or Gen Y (those born after 1981) represent an even larger segment with their numbers now eclipsing those of the boomers. The problem is this: For the boomers, 75 is the new 65. Boomers are healthier, living longer, identify themselves with careers, and they either don't want to or can't afford to retire into this down economy. So, at the same time Boomers aren't leaving the work force, the huge wave of Millennials is entering the workforce. This means that if you don't already have 50- and 60-year-olds working side-by-side with a 20-something—you will in the future.

As a leader you must learn to build bridges leading from old habits and comfort zones to the more fertile grounds of disruptive innovation. The best way to accomplish that is to align the creative energy of the younger generation, and the experience of your more seasoned workers with your organizational values and vision.

What I want to communicate is that you can run, but you cannot hide—sooner or later, knowingly or unknowingly, directly or indirectly, willingly or unwillingly, *every* leader must deal with the changing demographic shifts in the workforce. It impacts culture, performance, brand, innovation, leadership development, succession, and even the sustainability of your enterprise. As a leader you must get this right or fail.

Most of you understand what I'm sharing at a theoretical level—you've all looked at the numbers, and you've all studied the trends. That said, if you're honest, very few of you likely embrace these trends. And most of all, you probably don't leverage them on a day-to-day practical level, much less at a strategic level.

Let me give you an example of something that I observe regularly—the sad reality is that when I assess a new client's leadership team, it's the exception, not the rule, that youth has a seat at the table. And the real kicker is it's not because they don't have young talent, they simply don't know how to engage their younger talent.

These otherwise savvy leaders don't speak the same language, and they're frustrated. This often results in a disengaged, out of touch, *have always done it that way* leadership team. And when it comes time for succession, these organizations end up going outside the company to replace the old—old person, with a new old person. Not only are most companies building in leadership obsolescence, but they have no real idea of how to correct the problem, and they're certainly not leveraging the completely underutilized Gen X'rs and Gen Y'rs falling through the cracks of their company.

Here's my bottom line on the issue of age: If you don't have youth represented in your senior management and leadership teams, get some. Once they have a seat at the table, you also need to give them a voice. Now comes the really hard part . . . you then have to be willing to listen.

You won't ever engage younger workers, and you certainly won't unlock their creativity, passion, intelligence, and commitment if you don't respect them. Dismiss them, patronize them, or otherwise marginalize them, and they'll walk out the door. Show them you care about them, that you care about the right things—you know the small things like values, ethics, and transparency—and they'll be the fuel the runs your engine into the future. Failing to embrace this is the same thing as choosing to restrict your access to opportunity.

In summary, learn your business, and become very intentional about developing skills that will allow you to understand people—particularly people of influence (young and old). You cannot effectively lead those you don't know, have failed to understand, and have chosen not to serve.

The outcome of a leader's attempts at growing an organization, developing talent, and creating change will be rooted in his or her commitment to focus on changing themselves. I've often said it is impossible to create corporate growth without leadership growth or, put another way, you cannot scale an organization without scalable leadership. Become a better leader and you will not only be able to better predict the future, you will have the power to change it.

Chapter 4

Hacking the Mediocrity Gap

Leadership exists to disrupt mediocrity.

Question: Why is mediocrity so prevalent? Answer: It requires no courage. The best leaders exhibit the strength of character to move past the ordinary, usual, and customary, in order to reside in the realm of the extraordinary. They recognize that status quo thinking dulls the mind and lulls leaders into a false sense of security. I've always said the status quo is mediocrity's preferred weapon of choice. Great leaders must hack the mediocrity gap or face the consequences. Meritocracy or mediocrity—the choice is yours.

Take a moment and think about the talent and culture that exists in any organization you've worked for. It's not that hard to immediately conjure up images of mediocrity in people, process, systems, culture, and leadership. How sad is that? In fact, I'd go so far as to suggest most people wouldn't have trouble describing entire leadership teams, companies, and brands as mediocre. When excellence cedes its position to a lack thereof, even once-dominant companies will fall into decline.

In the opening paragraph of this chapter I mentioned mediocrity is so prevalent because it requires no courage. While a true statement to be sure, there's another reason; it often goes unnoticed. Leaders tend to notice the poor performers and the excellent performers, but mediocre performers simply tend to fly under the radar screen.

Pick a team, a product category, an industry vertical, or virtually any grouping by class and you'll find you can easily name the leaders and the laggers, but not the mediocre. You can name the winners and the losers, but rarely the runner-ups. Can you remember who finished second in the most recent Olympic 100 meter sprint? How about the runner-up in your last state senate race? When Jack Welch was selecting Jeffery Immelt to be his successor at GE, does anyone remember who it was Immelt beat out for the job? Is the name Reginald Jones familiar to you? That's the gentleman who preceded Welch as GE's CEO.

While this tendency is simply human nature, it's also very problematic for a leader.

How many of you remember studying the Pareto Principle (also known as the "law of the vital few" or the "80-20 rule") in school? The cause/effect theory credited to Vilfredo Pareto, an Italian economist, asks you to believe that in most cases 80 percent of the effects in a given area are created by 20 percent of the causes.

The business examples most commonly used to support this theory are that 80 percent of a company's sales are often generated by only 20 percent of its customers, or that 20 percent of a company's workforce produces 80 percent of the results. I would suggest that if you lead an organization with these ratios, you have not only left great amounts of unrealized potential on the table, but you have subjected your organization to greater risk, and have failed as a leader.

While these ratios hold true in certain instances, they are not universal, and they need not be accepted as the norm. Moreover, I would suggest where these ratios hold true, poor leadership is at work and mediocrity is alive and well. Too many leaders have bought into the Pareto Principle as an excuse to rationalize or justify mediocrity as opposed to understanding where operating leverage truly resides. Figure 4.1 shows us graphically what should just be common sense, but is often overlooked by leaders.

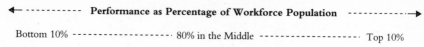

Figure 4.1   Performance as Percentage of Workforce Population

What this simple illustration demonstrates is that the potential for the biggest gains or losses in productivity/contribution occur in the middle of the spectrum with the largest segment of workforce population, and *not* at the ends of the range with the smallest numbers. Even if you raise the numbers at the ends of the spectrum to 20 percent and then reduce the middle to 60 percent, the middle is still where you find your greatest opportunity to generate operating leverage. The issue is not the percentage at the top or bottom, but what you do with the middle that matters most.

The truth is most organizations place their emphasis and their investments at either end of the spectrum and simply gloss over the bulk of their workforce. This does little more than result in lost opportunity costs, unrealized potential, increased turnover, and decreased morale. Leaders who don't hack the middle are sentencing their organizations to mediocrity.

When leaders tolerate anything less than a person's best effort, they do themselves, the individual in question, and everyone else a great disservice. They unknowingly set a negative precedent that others will gladly accept as suitable behavior. As my opening quote in this chapter states, a leader's job is to disrupt mediocrity.

Hacking the mediocrity gap requires rigor and discipline, and both these qualities begin and end with a leader's ability to focus. The good news is focus isn't really a skill as much as it is a decision. You either choose to focus, or you choose not to. A leader's ability to focus on purging mediocrity from their organization is one of the most valuable things they can do.

The best defense against mediocrity is not to let it get a toehold to begin with. Once it takes root in an organization, mediocrity will spread quickly, and become so entrenched that great amounts of time, effort, and expense will be required to eradicate it. Leaders become most susceptible to accepting mediocrity when distraction derails their focus.

Smart leaders don't wait until someone's been deemed at risk to implement triage, nor do they simply focus efforts on their high-potentials. Look at the entirety of your team as being high-potentials worthy of development, investment, and most of all, your attention.

Hacking the Impulsivity Gap

I have watched countless leaders suffer from self-inflicted wounds created by impulsivity. Do not confuse creativity with impulsiveness—they are not one in the same. Creativity is born from insightfulness, whereas impulsiveness is birthed by naïveté and/or arrogance. Ultimately it's a leader's lack of focus, or focus on the wrong area that allows impulsive thoughts to be acted upon.

In the last year alone we've observed our lawmakers shutdown the Federal Government; we saw Tom Armstrong, CEO of AOL, impulsively fire a senior employee on a public conference call; Netflix CEO Reed Hastings authorize a poorly conceived and ill-fated price increase; and Yahoo! CEO Marissa Mayer send a memo eliminating the ability for employees to work from home—and these are just a few examples.

We've all witnessed impulsive acts by leaders impact their performance, draw ridicule from the media, cost them their credibility, and in some cases even cost them their job. Whether it's politicians, military leaders, or chief executives, career suicide by impulsivity is alive and well.

Despite the old saying, people are *not* driven to distraction; they yield to it. Distraction is the most common cure for boredom. It paves the path of least resistance—it directs people to the easy way out. Distraction is often convenient, sometimes alluring, rarely beneficial, and usually leads to mediocrity.

One of the qualities I most admire in leaders is stability. The beautiful thing about stable leaders is they provide a stabilizing influence on others. They are leaders you can trust—they are leaders you can build around. Stable leaders model a level of constancy and consistency that individuals, teams, and organizations so desperately need, but often find missing.

Nik Wallenda recently became the first person to walk across the Little Colorado River Gorge near the Grand Canyon on a high wire without any support. What this seventh-generation member of the Flying Wallenda family so dramatically illustrated with his quarter-mile tight-rope walk 1,500 feet above the canyon floor is that stability matters.

Stability is something we don't often think about as a leadership quality—that is until it's absent. Think of the worst leaders you've encountered, and I can guarantee they were anything but stable. Erratic, ill-tempered, impulsive, or inconsistent leaders create unnecessary levels of operational tension, anxiety, and discord.

A lack of stability harms culture, stifles productivity, erodes trust, and makes it extremely difficult to retain top talent. Instability can also be a harbinger of bigger problems. The passing of time will usually reveal that unstable leaders tend to be lacking in several other areas.

Few things positively impact an organization like a stable tone from the top. A humble and resolute confidence, a sure hand, and a steady calm inspire belief in a leader's competence and capability. Stable leaders not only know where they stand, but they also leave no doubt in the minds of others as to what matters, and what will and won't be tolerated.

Stability was modeled for me for as long as I can remember. My father passed away this last year after a long illness, and of all the lessons he taught me over the years, one of the most valuable was the benefit of stability. I was raised in the same home until I left for college, he was married to my mother for 59 years, he practiced law for 47 years, and the wrist watch he was wearing on the day he died was the same timepiece his mother gave him for high school graduation. You knew what my father believed. Whether you agreed with him or not, he was dependable, and you could set your clock by him—he was nothing if not stable.

If you want to become a more stable leader, pay attention to the following four pillars of stability:

1. **True North:** Stable leaders have an open mind, but they also have strong convictions and principles. While stable leaders listen to others, they are not prone to being wishy-washy. Their values drive their actions—not the court of public opinion. You might not always agree with stable leaders, but you'll never have any doubt

as to where they stand. An aligned vision based upon clearly stated values, and the character to hold people accountable to values over outcomes create a high-trust culture. Purpose and people matter more than process and short-term results.

2. **You Play How You Practice:** Whether it's Nik Wallenda, a CEO, an educator, politician, or anyone else, your performance is always tied to your preparation. Training, development, and continuous life-long learning are the foundational cornerstones of stable leadership. A fake-it-until-you-make-it outlook is not only ill-conceived, it's often irresponsible, and usually doesn't end well.

3. **Lead with Compassion:** The most stable leaders understand their success is rooted in the care and well-being of those they lead. Stable leaders have a natural bias toward empathetic and compassionate behavior. When those you lead know you care, it creates a sense of trust and stability not found in more mercenary and callous leaders.

4. **Freedom to Fail:** If the people you lead are afraid to make mistakes, you'll never see their best work—you will have led them to perpetual state of mediocrity. Smart leaders make it safe for people to think big, take risks, and try new and different things. Nothing creates stability more than a high-trust environment where people are rewarded for the right behaviors—not punished for them.

Hacking the Impossibility Gap

How many times in your career have you heard someone say, "That's impossible—it simply can't be done." Perhaps you've even been guilty of uttering such a phrase yourself. Here's the thing—leaders don't accept impossibility as a valid thesis. If you think I've lost my mind, or that my optimistic nature has crossed over into a state of irrational exuberance or delusion, I'd encourage you to read on as I challenge the logic of impossibility.

The fact something has yet to be accomplished is rarely evidence of impossibility, rather it usually means whatever "it" is just hasn't happened yet. Put simply, a lack of a particular outcome signals a lack of accomplishment, not impossibility. History has proven time and again that incurable diseases become curable, so-called laws of science are revealed to have been little more than flawed theory, and physical limitations once believed insurmountable are eventually exceeded.

When leaders view everything through a lens of *what is*, they often get a false positive on impossibility. However when they change to a filter of *what if*, the barriers to possibility are often removed. Conventional wisdom will tell you attainment and achievement lead to great outcomes. However, true wisdom reveals that discovery leads to better outcomes. Great leaders don't play to an end, they think beyond outcomes—do you?

What if Michelangelo, Einstein, Ford, or the Wright Brothers had settled for impossibility over possibility? What if Gates, Jobs, and Bezos had focused on *what was* instead of the possibilities of *what could be*? What if our next generation of researchers, scientists, entrepreneurs, and academics fail to challenge conventional thinking? What if our world leaders continue to view the status quo as acceptable? As a society we cannot afford to embrace theory as fact, fiction as truth, or good enough as good enough. The burden and privilege of leadership simply demand more.

When you think about what keeps good leaders up at night, it's rarely an issue of *can* things be done, but more likely an issue of *should* they be done? Given enough time and resources, virtually anything can be accomplished. If you say you don't have the resources, I will surmise you're not very resourceful. If you state you don't have the time, I will conclude you're not very focused. If you imply you have too many things on your plate, I have no choice but to believe you're not very disciplined.

Where the absence of an outcome or a discovery exists so does a lack of creativity, critical thought, focused energy, effort and resources, and ultimately a lack of leadership. My thesis is a simple one: "The plausibility of impossibility only becomes a probability in the absence of leadership." Leadership is the difference between what could have been and what will be.

Leaders must refuse to accept the status quo. Consider this—if nobody ever reinvented the wheel, the tires we drive around on would still be made out of stone. Whenever I see leaders focus on maintenance over innovation, I see people who have unnecessarily drawn the line of impossibility in the sand. As I've stated before, a leader's job is to disrupt mediocrity—not embrace it, to challenge the norm—not embolden it, to weed out apathy—not reward it, and to dismantle bureaucracies—not build them.

Hacking the Safety Gap

One of mediocrity's greatest protectors can be found in the rationalization of safe behaviors and decisions. The thought of "safe" might be a comforting term, but it's also a relative term. Safe leaders prefer the known to the unknown, thought over action, rules over guidelines, and the brake over the accelerator. Safe leaders hide in the comfort of their own opinions rather than seek out the challenge of dissenting opinion and fresh ideas.

Here's the thing—I've found safe decisions rarely are. Great leaders possess the courage to not only seek out the right decision, but they also understand the importance of giving others permission to do the same. We need leaders who want others to do better and be better. What we don't need is more leaders who hide in safe harbors. Leaders don't get paid to make safe decisions; they get paid to make the right decision.

It's also important to understand safe decisions are not universally synonymous with smart decisions. In fact, most times the safe decision is a rationalization or justification that attempts to provide cover for what is knowingly a less than optimal choice. Have you ever noticed how weak leaders will often opt for the easy decision while the best leaders have learned to make the tough decisions look easy?

Leaders whose default setting is to play it safe do not impress me. The issue with the aforementioned statement is many will read it as being unduly harsh—therein lies the problem. Organizations have incubated a generation of leaders who believe their job is to make safe decisions, when in fact their job is to make good decisions.

I'm not suggesting decisions be made with reckless abandon, but neither do I believe every decision needs to be hedged, every expectation needs to be lowered, or every constituency needs to be pandered to. While good decisions measure and manage risk, they are rarely risk free. Leaders who look for risk-free decisions do little more than cede opportunity to others.

Following are five types of decisions that many see as the safe decision—savvy leaders understand they're anything but safe:

1. **The Politically Correct Decision:** Smart leaders don't seek to be politically correct—they seek to be correct. Being politically correct rarely solves problems—it exacerbates them. Real change, not the politically correct version, is built upon seeking the truth, and not some watered-down version thereof. The first step in solving problems is to deal in whole truths, not untruths or partial truths.

2. **The Talent Decision:** I can't even begin to count the number of times I've witnessed organizations make the safe hire instead of the right hire. The reason companies make bad hires is they compromise, they settle, they play it safe—they don't hire the *best person* for the job. Compromise has its place in business, but it has no role in the acquisition of talent. Leaders too often focus on the "nice to haves" instead of the "must haves." They allow themselves to be distracted by disparate, insignificant factors, rather than holding out for the best person for the job. My definition of irony: when leaders complain about their talent. I've always believed leaders deserve the teams they build. Here's the thing—when leaders make a bad hire they have no one to blame but themselves. If you don't believe you can hire world-class talent, don't be surprised when others begin to share your opinion.

3. **The Values Decision:** Rewarding performance over values might seem to be safe or smart, but it is neither. Organizations have core values for a reason—to give them a true north. Organizational values exist to align interests, actions, and direction. Ultimately they exist to create a high-trust environment where exceptional performance is the rule and not the exception. When leaders make decisions that contradict core values, there is a steep price to pay—a loss of trust. When a leaders talks about values, but fails to act on or defend them, the entire enterprise is placed at risk. The best leaders have a zero tolerance policy for actions and/or decisions that constitute a violation of corporate values.

4. **The Managed Decision:** Many leaders believe if they can manage enough aspects of a decision, then it will be safe to make. When decisions are overmanaged they tend to be undereffective.

Leaders need to stop managing decisions and just make them. I've always said, "Managing expectations is gamesmanship—aligning them is leadership." Smart leaders offer a compass; they don't draw the map. Think guidelines—not rules. Think surrender—not control. Build the right team, and have the confidence to allow decisions to be made closest to the point of impact.

5. **The No Decision:** While it may seem safe to not make a decision, it's probably not. The reality is, not making a decision is still a decision—it's usually just not the right decision. Avoiding a decision doesn't mean you'll avoid the issue; you'll likely just exacerbate it. Great leaders don't find safety by sticking their head in the sand; they find safety in consistently making good decisions. However, the greatest security is found by teaching others to make great decisions and then granting them the responsibility and authority to make them.

Hacking Political Correctness

I mentioned politically correct decisions above, but of even greater concern is the spread of politically correct thinking into every aspect of our lives. The institutionalization of politically correct thinking has done more to harm operating businesses than just about any other social and/or cultural influence in recent times.

I don't know about you, but it's almost as if we've raised a generation of leaders who feel they have a moral and ethical obligation to be politically correct—*wrong*. Their responsibility is to be correct; not politically correct. The harsh truth is politically correct thinking is a large contributor to an increase in mediocre behavior, a decrease in workplace productivity, and of greater concern, to the moral and ethical decay of our society. Are these extreme statements? Perhaps some may think so, but being authentic to my politically incorrect self, I think not.

What's troubling to me, and I hope to you, is that politically correct assault has invaded classrooms; the media; the work place; federal, state, and local government; the judiciary; the church; the military; and even casual discussions with friends and family. It has spread to pandemic proportions, crossing boarders and cultures, such that you'd be hard pressed to actually find organizations where tough, candid conversations frequently take place without HR mediating them.

Few things will send morale and productivity into decline faster than leadership that adopts a politically correct mind-set. Before those of dissenting (politically correct) opinions become too outraged with my position, let me be perfectly clear; I believe strongly in respect and compassion. These characteristics should be present in all human beings. They are admirable qualities so long as they don't take precedence over, ignore, or contradict truth.

The main problem with politically correct thinking is that it confuses kindness and courtesy with bureaucratic mandates, and ends up stripping people of their real opinions. I'm not advocating being mean-spirited, arrogant, judgmental, or self-righteous—quite to the contrary. It is very possible, and preferable, to have truth and compassion co-exist *without* being subject to political correctness.

Think about it; wouldn't it be more prudent to let the facts and/or the truth surrounding a particular matter to rise above the rhetoric and guide your actions rather than to blindly adopt an attitude of political correctness? Of course it would—except for one huge problem: In the face of perceived conflict, dissension, threats, or controversy, people tend to default to denial, justification, and rationalization. In today's politically correct world, it is just easier for most people to hide in the safety of the majority than it is to take on the risk of being outspoken, innovative, disruptive, challenging, convicted, bold, controversial, or truthful. Therein lies the problem with political correctness.

By its very nature, politically correct thinking is most often disingenuous, if not altogether intellectually dishonest. Politically correct thinking replaces individuality and authentic opinions with socially acceptable rhetoric and watered-down behavioral tendencies. I actually miss the days when most conversations consisted of unpredictable, highly charged, and stimulating discourse where people were encouraged to openly share their true thoughts and opinions.

The irony of politically correct thinking is that a society void of individual thought actually creates the opposite of diversity. It is in fact politically correct thinking that results in a brainwashed group of sheep that completely lack diversity as a result of a generification of thoughts and actions. The dark secret behind politically correct thinking is that it slowly dulls your senses, and neuters your innate ability to be discerning.

I don't know about you, but I don't want to hear what you think I want you to say, or what you think you should say, but rather I want to hear what you're really thinking. Have you ever sat in a meeting where all parties sit around the table with a deer in the headlights look trying to figure out how to dance around an issue rather than address it head-on? It is this type of issue that pollutes our culture, stifles innovation, undermines our productivity, and sentences those who embrace politically correct thinking to a life of mediocrity.

Taking a politically correct stance simply shows a person values comfort and safety more than truth. The sad reality is many people believe so strongly that there is safety in numbers they will compromise their own thoughts, and ultimately their integrity by adopting a *safe* position, rather than take the risk of standing strongly for their beliefs. It has become more important to "do things right" rather than to "do the right things." Blending in has become in vogue, while making waves via independent thinking has become labeled as socially inappropriate behavior.

In the end, leaders that adopt a politically correct stance place themselves and their organizations at great peril. You cannot be an effective leader subordinating right thinking to popular thinking. Diversity of thought is critical to the success of any enterprise presupposing one requisite—that it is honest thought. While smart leaders won't tolerate a culture built on the "yes man" approach to business, neither will they tolerate politically correct thinking. Real leaders like to be challenged—they want to be inspired by new ideas and creative thoughts. They are even willing to put up with running down a few rabbit trails in the pursuit of innovation as long as efforts are based upon honesty, candor, and the good of the overall organization.

So, back to the original question. . . . How do I feel about political correctness in the workplace? My world, albeit I'm in the minority in my perspective, is one where humility, respect, and compassion are required, excellence is demanded, and politically correct behavior is not tolerated. A generic thought, ambivalence, attempting to fly under the radar, and mediocre performance will definitely get my attention (not in a good way). If you don't make waves and challenge the status quo you're not giving your best—you're just phoning it in.

The best leaders don't play it safe, they don't look the other way when something is wrong, and they don't compromise on values. They do the right thing. Doing the right thing means *never* settling for mediocrity.

Chapter 5

Hacking the Culture Gap

Leadership not accountable to its people, will
eventually be held accountable by its people.

F ew things are more critical to leadership success than building a healthy, aligned culture. As obvious as this should be to anyone, far too many leaders still don't get it. I never cease to be amazed at how many leaders talk about culture, without actually doing anything to improve culture. Understanding how to hack cultural gaps can make the difference between success and failure.

Let me be as clear as I can—the phrase "toxic work environment" is code for bad leadership. Toxic work environments can only exist where a lack of trust and respect are present, and this can only occur in the absence of sound leadership. The reality is a toxic culture simply cannot co-exist in the presence of great leadership.

A toxic work environment thrives off of everything great leadership stands in opposition to. The fuel for toxicity is conflict not resolution, ego not humility, self-interest not service above self, gossip and innuendo not truth, social and corporate climbing not team-building, and the list could go on. Toxic cultures occur where arrogance, ignorance, ambivalence, and apathy are present, but again, not where steady leadership stands at the helm.

Great corporate cultures are intentional—they are built by design. While I suppose that a great culture could somehow evolve by default or osmosis, I have yet to observe it. Creating a healthy culture is a matter of making it a focus point within the corporate values, purpose, vision, mission, and strategy. Put simply, a corporation's strategy that ignores, or only pays lip service to culture, will be the beneficiary of the unhealthy environment they deserve.

Even if an organization *lucks* its way into a good culture, I would suggest it would not be sustainable without being part of the core business strategy. Culture formed by the moment, will also change by the moment, and ultimately it will disappear in a moment.

Hacking the Gap between Strategy and Culture

So, where does culture fit into the corporate landscape, and how important is it? Culture is a construct that must be embedded into the very fabric of the corporate identity. It must be part of the ethos that describes *why* the enterprise exists, *what* and *who* it values, and *how* it will behave. But it must also be much more than that—it must embody the very pulse of the business—it must be a living, breathing heartbeat that leaders, employees, customers, and other stakeholders can visibly feel. More importantly, culture must be something they want to identify with and be a part of.

Because of everything mentioned above, a healthy culture can be a competitive advantage or the very thing that can bring ruin upon a business. Leaders have clearly awakened to the fact that culture matters. And it's about time. Culture is critically important to the success of any enterprise. That said, like any trend, too much of a good thing can spin out of control and become destructive.

This is why culture must be created from a design perspective—it must be intentional and purposeful. It must be part of an openly expressed and understood honor code that guides talent acquisition, development, compensation, and deployment. It must be part of the strategy that dictates acceptable behaviors, how decisions will be made, and what will drive operational focus.

Where culture becomes dangerous is when it remains in the ethereal. When culture is not understood, not integrated, not led, and allowed to be amorphous, it can spin out of control. Culture can become distracting or, even worse, destructive. Where the world stands today reminds me quite a bit of the pre-bubble early days of the dot-com era.

Back in the dot-com days I watched many a young enterprise suffer from placing culture ahead of strategy or, worse, even focusing on culture in lieu of strategy. When the marketplace began to see through the spin and the vapor, all the Ping-Pong tables and funky offices in the world couldn't save a flawed business model. The fun was over, and the culture ceased to exist.

The sad reality is that culture run amok can kill companies. Many a company has put so much emphasis on culture that culture simply became their business as opposed to strengthening and guiding their business. All the perks and benefits in the world won't cause a company to thrive if not guided by purpose, governed by sound core values, and wrapped into a vision that can be strategically and tactically implemented.

Business should be fun. The workplace should be comfortable and secure, and time spent on the job should add value to a person's life. Culture is important—it is very important. But if culture is developed outside of strategy, if it's not driven by strategy, then said culture will likely become little more than a very dangerous intoxicant.

Every vibrant, healthy, inspiring, innovative, and positive corporate culture I've witnessed has occurred not because culture has been placed ahead of strategy, but because it has been a key driver of the corporate strategy. Why does everything in today's world have to be framed within an exclusionary either/or proposition? I've consistently found that the best scenarios are the ones that allow you to have your cake and eat it too. Why separate culture from strategy to their mutual demise, when culture is secured, enhanced, and sustained by sound strategy? It's not really strategy *versus* culture, but an aligned strategy *and* culture that matter.

As I mentioned above, culture isn't an accident. It's either created by design or default. Let's examine a company universally known for their strength of culture—Apple. The simple truth of the matter is Apple works at culture. The Apple culture didn't happen by osmosis; it was and is engineered by design. Steve Jobs was nothing if not a cultural zealot. His vision, values, passions, and pursuits were not only clearly articulated, they were seamlessly interwoven into the business model, and strictly adhered to. Apple employees who didn't buy-off on the Apple cultural ethos were simply weeded out.

It's important to remember that while culture exists from day one, it takes time to gel. Apple was not an overnight success, nor was its culture. It took decades of purposed, intentional, and unyielding focus to create the Apple culture that exists today. Culture must be fought for on a daily basis, and it must continue to evolve in order to become better, stronger, and healthier. If you lose the culture battle you'll lose the talent battle, the brand battle, and the eventually the sustainability battle.

I challenge you to name a single category dominant brand, or even a hot up-and-coming brand where the culture doesn't flow through the strategy, to the business model, and eventually to the consumer/ end-user.

The Right Foundation—Hacking the Culture Construct

I'm confident anyone reading this book understands the value of culture—it's not too hard to reach consensus on this point. But when it comes to agreeing upon the best construct for building a healthy, thriving, and sustainable culture, the opinions are varied, and the discussions are nothing short of spirited.

I've had the opportunity to witness a myriad of what I'll refer to as *cultural engineering experiments*—some more successful than others. While everyone seems to have an opinion on how to build a successful culture, most leaders overcomplicate the matter, and they often miss some of the most basic steps.

When you think about culture, it's less about complex frameworks and more about people. Healthy cultures can't be built by setting boundaries, through the enforcement of arbitrary rules or bureaucratic mandates, and you certainly can't manage culture by instituting intricate processes. Culture shouldn't be imposed upon people—as cocreators of the culture, the people are the culture.

What I want you to take away from this section is that culture is not something to be managed, but rather something to be led. All attempts to manage culture are doomed from the start; eventually requiring triage and reengineering. Efforts at leading culture have a huge upside, and the best chance of sustainability over the long haul. As Table 5.1 demonstrates, managing culture (old paradigm) is not nearly as effective as leading culture (new paradigm).

Hacking the Management Construct

I'm probably just as tired as you are of the management vs. leadership debate. Most rational people understand leadership and management are at their respective bests when they coexist and work in collaboration. That said, I think it's also fair to say recent history shows that most organizations have operated in an environment far too heavily weighted toward the management side of the equation.

As Table 5.1 demonstrates, we have managed culture to the extent businesses have created a culture of management when what they really need is a culture of leadership. When culture is led, and a culture of leadership is embraced, the benefits of sound management are not lost; they are simply enhanced by a broader perspective. I've always said, "A great leader can accomplish much, but a culture of leadership can accomplish much more."

A culture of leadership replaces rigid frameworks with loose communities of collaborative networks. Complex decisions are not reserved for someone sitting atop a hierarchical structure, but are driven down and across the organization. Think open-source not proprietary, adaptive not static, actionable not theoretical, and progressive not regressive.

The best way to create a culture of leadership is to value and reward authentic and effective leadership. Create a culture based upon an ethos

Table 5.1 Old Paradigm versus New Paradigm

Old Paradigm—Managing Culture	New Paradigm—Leading Culture
Have a Leader	Create a Culture of Leadership
Invest in Tools	Invest in People
Follow "Best Practices"	Develop "Next Practices"
Punish Failure	Encourage Risk
Play the Game	Change the Game
Compete	Collaborate
Driven by Profit Agenda	Driven to Create Value
Discourage Independent Thinking	Embrace Dissenting Opinion
Start with "What"	Start with "Why"
Place People in Boxes	Free People from Boxes
Protect the Status Quo	Challenge Everything
Trivialize Youth	Give Youth a Seat at the Table
Reward Potential	Reward Contribution
Ideate	Innovate
Complex Decisions Controlled at the Top	Complex Decision Driven to the Edges
Message	Engage
Have a Plan	Have a Purpose
Leverage their People	Create Leverage for their People
Quick to Say "No"	Find a Way to Get to a "Yes"
Optics	Ethics
Manage Risk	Manage Opportunity
Set Boundaries	Close Gaps
Train	Develop
Destination Mentality	Continuum Mentality
Assign Blame	Accept Responsibility
Manage Expectations	Align Expectations
Think Span of Control	Think Span of Influence
Goal Driven	Discovery Driven
Focus on "Who" is Right	Focus on "What" is Right
Observe	Understand

that empowers, attracts, differentiates, and sustains. Remember this: The only culture that flourishes over the long haul is a culture of leadership.

Hacking the Scarcity Gap

Do you work in an environment that fosters leadership at every level, or just at the top of the org chart? You can either chasten people for attempting to lead, or encourage them to take risks, to explore opportunities, and to make decisions. If you want to create a culture of leadership, you must succeed in creating leadership ubiquity.

I write and speak often on the value of creating a culture of leadership, yet I continue to be amazed at how many organizations simply fail to understand the impossibility of creating such a culture when people are consistently told they're not leaders. Organizations built on the backs of weak dependent followers aren't nearly as vibrant or sustainable as those designed through the collaborative efforts of strong independent leaders.

If you take one thing away from this section let it be this: Leadership that isn't transferrable, repeatable, scalable, and sustainable isn't really leadership at all. Not everyone can be the CEO, but everyone can lead. Ponder this next statement for a moment: If you believe you're not a leader, don't be surprised when others begin to agree with you.

When in doubt, think ubiquity not scarcity. Leadership isn't, or at least shouldn't be, a scarce commodity. Far too many companies wrongly treat leadership as an esoteric role reserved for a privileged few. However, healthy organizations realize leadership must be a ubiquitous quality that pervades every aspect of day-to-day operations. They understand every person must lead; even if people are only responsible for leading themselves, they must lead.

The problem with what I've espoused thus far is found in the reality of how society has changed our perception of leadership through the years. The devolution of leadership as a practice has occurred as a result of two primary items: (1) the abdication of personal responsibility and accountability by many in the workforce, and (2) the hijacking of authority and control by those who value self-promotion and power above real leadership.

Any individual who holds responsibility for any person, aspect, function, or task within an organization is in fact a leader. You may not be in charge, but if your direct or indirect efforts influence others, you are in fact leading. The higher up the org chart you reside, the more dependent you are on the leadership ability of those you lead. Anyone who offers advice, creative thought, input, or feedback is helping to shape the perceptions of senior leaders—such people also thereby function as leaders themselves.

When we fail to accept our responsibility as co-workers and citizens, when we so easily cede our authority to others, we not only fail to lead—we sentence ourselves to a life of squandered potential. Keep in mind that the people with the greatest formal authority do not necessarily possess or exert the greatest influence.

The reality is the only person who can strip you of leadership is you. The best leaders not only lead themselves well, they also develop others to become highly skilled leaders. They're not threatened by the success of others, but take great satisfaction in it.

While there are always exceptions to any rule, you'll find it difficult to point to more than a small handful of successful leaders who don't understand what I've just espoused. The best leaders don't view what they do as a job, they see it as a calling. Their passion is to help others to grow, develop, and become better. Think of the best leaders you know, and I'll guarantee you they spend the bulk of their time building into others. I'd encourage you to do the same.

Hacking the Courage Gap

Creating a culture of leadership is not for the faint of heart—it takes great courage. It takes great courage to break from the norm, challenge the status quo, seek new opportunities, cut your losses, make the tough decision, listen rather than speak, admit your faults, forgive the faults of others, not allow failure to dampen your spirit, stand for those not capable of standing for themselves, and remain true to your core values. You can do none of these things without courage. Courage is having the strength of conviction to do the right thing when it would be easier to do things right.

Courage is a trait possessed by all great leaders. So much so, that leadership absent courage is nothing short of a farce. Let me be very clear—I'm not advocating for bravado, arrogance, or an overabundance of hubris, but the courage necessary to stay the course and to do the right things. Standing behind decisions that everyone supports doesn't particularly require a lot of chutzpah. On the other hand, standing behind what one believes is the right decision in the face of tremendous controversy is the stuff great leaders are made of. I believe it was Aristotle who referred to courage as the *first virtue*, because it makes all of the other virtues possible.

The best thing about courage is that a lack of it can be overcome. Courage is teachable, and therefore it is learnable—proof of this can be found in every instance of overcoming a fear. Courage should not be defined as the absence of fear—that's ignorance. Courage is finding the strength to move ahead in the presence of fear. In short, courage isn't a skill; it is a decision. Think of courage as a muscle that needs to be developed and exercised. Strong muscles atrophy without use, and so will your courage.

Here's the thing—we'll all be remembered for the decisions we make or don't make, and the courage we display or we fail to exercise. Leaders who consistently demonstrate courage will stand apart from the masses, and earn the trust and loyalty of those they lead. As a general rule, most people can be characterized by their courage or their lack thereof:

- In the corporate world those who demonstrate courage stand apart as innovators and opinion leaders, those who display a lack of courage are viewed as yes men who are the politically correct defenders of status quo.
- In the military great courage is often referred to as heroism, while a lack of courage will brand you a coward.
- On the stage of world affairs those who display courage are statesmen, and those who don't are politicians.
- In relationships, courage will show you to be a trusted friend, whereas the absence of courage will reveal you as a gossip, adversary, or even enemy.

Each day brings with it a new set of challenges, and the best any of us can hope for is that we will have the courage and character to stand behind our personal beliefs and convictions, regardless of public opinion or outcome. Courage will make you faithful, where a lack of courage will cause you to be fearful. Whether you look back on your personal experience or a greater historical reference, you'll find it is always better to stand for courage than regret failing to do so.

Hacking the Arrogance Gap

A culture of leadership simply cannot exist where egos are allowed to run unchecked. All leaders have blind spots, and blind spots simply pose potential areas of vulnerability. However not all blind spots are created equal. Few things create areas of risk for leaders like their own sense of pride and ego. Here's the thing—leaders' desire to have their ego stroked makes them vulnerable to a very seductive form of manipulation—flattery.

The most common form of manipulation comes packaged in the form of flattery—it's also the most dangerous. The veil of most hidden agendas are also typically cloaked in flattery. The insidious nature of flattery is that it becomes most powerful when it is served to those who thirst for it. Leaders who place their need for adoration and acclaim above serving the needs of others are high value targets for those who would abuse the trust given to them.

If you take one thing away from this section, it should be this—the power that comes with a leader's ability to positively influence others is only trumped by the power given away as others adversely influence them. If you've been around long enough, you're probably aware the silent assassin of many a leader is flattery.

The problem with the old saying that "flattery will get you everywhere" is that those with less than pure intentions not only believe it, they act on it. The lazy, the power hungry, the greedy, the gravy-trainers, the psychopaths, and the sociopaths all understand that flattery is *not* harmless. Quite to the contrary, these soothsayers understand that flattery has the power to influence, corrupt, undermine, and deceive—they wield flattery as a lethal weapon against the undiscerning. Manipulation in the form of flattery is little more than a covert form of aggression.

Before I go any further it is important to understand that *praise* and *flattery*, while often used interchangeably, are not synonymous. "Praise" is most commonly defined as the expression of favorable judgment or sincere appreciation. "Flattery" is most commonly defined as excessive and insincere praise. The naïve, the needy, the impressionable, or the egocentric view flattery as genuine praise. Discerning people understand flattery to be disingenuous, false praise motivated by an agenda.

Here's the thing—in times past it was a bit easier to discern authentic praise from false praise because the methods by which relationships were constructed was different. We used to build our relationships slowly and carefully based upon personal history and experience.

Trust was earned over time through personal observations of a person's character, actions, and decisions. Ah, the good old days. . . .

In today's digital world, speed has influenced every aspect of our lives—perhaps most notably how we build our relationships and whom we grant access to. If you examine the speed at which people acquire their friends, fans, followers, and connections on social networks, and how they market themselves and their companies using social media, you'll find many seem to be in a race to include as many people in their spheres of influence as possible. The only barrier to entry for inclusion in most people's networks today seems to be that they are *polite*. Let me be clear—I have nothing against polite behavior so long as it's not accompanied by a hidden agenda.

How often have you received adulation from the overly effusive in the form of an e-mail, blog comment, tweet, or Facebook message from people you hardly know, and how does that make you feel? Do you trust them? Do you trust their motives? It's as if the currency of social networking is rapidly becoming flattery—it should be trust. I'm not interested in flattery, but sincerity. It was Socrates who said, "Think not those faithful who praise thy words and actions but those who kindly reprove thy faults." What leaders need to become cognizant of is that flattery comes with the territory. The more influence you have, the more you'll be prone to attract flattery. The question is, can you discern fact from fiction and can you handle it?

This is one of my favorite quotes from Martin Luther: "The ears of our generation have been made so delicate by the senseless multitude of flatterers that, as soon as we perceive anything of ours is not approved of, we cry out that we are being bitterly assailed; and when we can repel the truth by no other pretense, we escape by attributing bitterness, impatience, intemperance, to our adversaries." Things really haven't changed too much have they?

Hacking the Rumor Mill

If flattery is the silent assassin of leaders, then so is gossip the silent assassin of culture. Let me cut right to the chase—real leaders don't participate in gossip, and likewise they don't tolerate gossip from others. Gossip destroys trust, assails credibility, and is one of the greatest adversaries of a healthy corporate culture. The emotional distress and political discord associated with gossip undermines workplace performance, and can be nothing short of disastrous. In the text that follows I'll share my thoughts on how to control gossip in the workplace.

My question for leaders is this: Do you want to create a culture of doubt or a culture of leadership? If what you desire is to have a healthy, thriving, and productive company, it is essential that you curtail office gossip. Gossip is one of the most divisive undercurrents pervading business today. Gossip allows the unnecessary dispersion of negative innuendo for the pleasure of a few, and to the detriment of many. Show me a person that participates in gossip, and I'll show you someone who cannot be trusted. People who participate in gossip often times view their activity as being politically savvy when in fact gossip is the tool of insecure, rank amateurs.

It's actually been trendy of late to take the position that participating in gossip affords opportunities to gather business intelligence, build relationships, and so on. While these theories make for nice sound bites, they are at best a big stretch. In reality, they do little more than constitute more rhetoric attempting to rationalize and justify poor character. If you have to participate in gossip to feel plugged-in, liked, or informed, then your leadership ability is woefully lacking.

I've written often on the importance of building solid relationships through displaying a consistency of character, creating a bond of trust, making good decisions, and striving to help others succeed. When you take part in gossip, you do none of these things. In fact, gossip seriously undermines each one of the aforementioned success metrics by propagating inaccurate information. At its core, gossip is the highest form of disloyalty, and it is far from innocent or idle. Nothing can claim more tainted professional reputations, destroyed friendships, and polluted corporate cultures than gossip.

The best definition I've found for gossip is: "talking about a situation with somebody who is neither a part of the solution nor a part of the problem." If you have a problem with a person, or take exception to a particular situation, go directly to the source. There are few things in life I loathe as much as those that don't have the courage and integrity to hit things head on. If I have a problem with people, I give them the courtesy and respect of addressing the issue with them in private. Talking to anyone else wouldn't resolve the issue, it would merely be self-serving indulgence at someone else's expense. In fact, it is my opinion that the worst form of gossip is often conducted under the guise of seeking advice or counsel. If you need to seek the wisdom of a third party prior to addressing the root issue, do it generically and anonymously so as not to impugn the character of another.

To be clear, I'm not recommending the stifling of healthy discourse. I have nothing against forms of communication that are good-natured, inspiring, impassioned, productive, healthy, educational, informational, effective, and so on. Most organizations have a history, and with history comes the mystique of folklore and legend. Every culture has stories to be told, heroes to be adored, villains to be chastened, and a variety of characters to be acknowledged. The key is the intention behind the communication—is it meant to help or hurt, to advance or undermine, to build up or tear down? Gossip is simply not to be confused with other forms of communication—they are not one and the same.

Don't fall prey to the delusion that leaking gossip online via social media is any less harmful or somehow different—it's not. It's perfectly fine to debate positional differences, but it's not okay to attack someone personally because of a positional difference. If you feel the need to attack or belittle someone, take the discussion offline as it's not appropriate for a public forum.

As I mentioned above, gossip isn't idle, nor is it innocent, cute, or something to be trivialized as insignificant. At best gossip creates unnecessary tension, but most often it creates outright conflict. As a leader, you wouldn't likely tolerate gossip targeted at you, so if you allow gossip to be spread about others, what does this say about you? If gossip pervades your organization and you are not aware of it, then you clearly don't have the pulse of your organization, your public statements about the importance of culture and morale will seem disingenuous, and you're likely guilty of being what I refer to as a disconnected leader.

In the same fashion that being the source of gossip is destructive, so is furthering the damage by ratcheting up the rhetoric by participating in gossip. If someone comes to you about a problem with another person, immediately redirect that individual back to the person in question. If that doesn't work, and you must get involved, offer to accompany the person with the problem in addressing the individual they have an issue with. As a leader it is much more productive to aid in the solution rather than foster the problem.

I have watched many a well-intentioned executive get sucked into gossip in an attempt to help, only to pay a big price down the road for this error in judgment. If you want to be a long-term survivor in business, I would suggest that you not participate in gossip and get rid of those that do. Remember that those individuals that will gossip to you, will also gossip about you.

Many would suggest that the thought of eliminating gossip in the corporate world is an exercise in naïveté. They would take the position that gossip is just part of human nature, and that gossip will always exist in any type of environment where social dynamics are present. The old saying "It is what it is" is only true until you decide to make a difference. As a leader, it is incumbent upon you to do the right thing, which is to protect your reputation and those that you work with. Furthermore, allowing anyone under your charge to participate in any activity to the contrary makes you an accomplice in the decline of morale, and the decay of your corporate culture. Put simply, good leaders don't tolerate gossip—they eradicate it.

If you're still inclined to partake in gossip let me leave you with the following three thoughts:

1. No worthwhile gain ever comes at another's unjust expense.
2. It's more profitable to do your own work than to tear down or lay claim to the work of others.
3. Envy and deceit never give birth to lasting joy.

The lesson here is that culture matters—forget this and all other efforts with regard to talent initiatives will be dysfunctional, if not lost altogether.

Hacking Diversity

There is no doubt diversity is a tricky issue, but likely not for the reasons many believe. My belief is too much diversity exists for the wrong reasons, and not enough diversity exists for the right reasons. Much of what I'll share in this section runs completely counter to politically correct sentiments, but doesn't run afoul of sound leadership doctrine.

I have really grown quite weary of the "Diversity" debate. Let me be clear: A leader's job is not to build a diverse culture, but a rich and productive culture—they are not always one and the same. I can't really think of any issue that should be argued or decided solely on the merits of diversity. In fact, let me take it up even another notch . . . with the exception of seeking diversity of thought, approach, and perspective, diversity should be a non-issue altogether.

Those of you familiar with my writing know that I often take the unpopular side of an issue if I believe it worthy of mention. I do not shy away from pointing out things that should be common sense for business people, which need to be publicly stated, but rarely are.

It is not my intent to offend anyone with the text that follows, and if you find yourself being offended, it is my opinion you need to examine your motives and principles. The issues of diversity in business when handled properly can be catalysts for growth. However, this is not the case in most instances, and as a result, diversity has become one of the leading killers of corporate productivity.

Let's start with a reality check . . . there is no doubt that we live in a diverse world. Unless you live on an isolated mountain top, without access to other people or the media at large, it would be difficult to get through the day without being impacted by issues of ethnicity, race, gender, age, sexual preference, religion, physical appearance, mental and physical challenges, and so on. However from my perspective, the issue is not whether we recognize diversity, but rather how it is dealt with. . . .

I have no problem whatsoever with the concept of equal opportunity, so long as it is not misunderstood, misapplied, or mandated. You will never see me deny that all human beings are created equal, and that those of us in the United States are recognized to have been endowed with certain unalienable rights. However I refuse to make business decisions that are not in the best interests of the business, simply to appeal to the wrong groups for the wrong reasons.

Don't make your case by playing the diversity card, play the I'm qualified card. Compete on your merits, not why your lack thereof should be overlooked. If you're not qualified don't try to work around your lack of qualifications, go get the qualifications you need to compete.

In evaluating any person/relationship, smart leaders look for value, talent, performance, leverage, efficiency, economy of scale, work ethic, integrity, character, discipline, and many other traits irrespective of your skin color, age, and so on. I care about your contribution to the enterprise at every level—not just culturally. I don't mean to downplay culture, as a diverse corporate culture is something to be strived for, but only if quality is not sacrificed. The best leaders refuse to lower the chinning bar by allowing for the hiring of someone based more on their diversity segment than their talent.

The secret to diversity is to find people who share your vision, but bring a different set of relevant professional and life experiences to the table. Real diversity is hiring a self-starter who grew up poor and built his own business when the rest of your team all went to Wharton. Or a person who grew up in New York City when your team is all from the Midwest, and you need to appeal to urban clients. Hiring a woman with a different skin color who is in every way exactly like the rest of your team isn't getting you anything special. You can see this on the Supreme Court, where presidents often select a groupthink person who just checks the right diversity boxes, but only Scalia and Sotomayor think truly differently than everyone else.

Diversity mandates just don't work. Talent begets talent, and blending occurs naturally when good decisions are made for the right reasons. When you force the diversity agenda for the wrong reasons (no matter how well intended), productivity suffers, and resentment grows.

The simple truth is that lowering standards is never a good thing in any environment. A sense of entitlement is not a substitute for work ethic and a desire to achieve. By maintaining the highest of standards, you force people to raise their game and be the best that they can be. Anything other than this fosters unhealthy dependencies that bring out the worst in people, and not the best they have to offer.

Allow me to share my personal philosophy on the topic of diversity. It is a nonissue, because I don't make personal or business decisions based upon social mandates or politically correct thinking. Over the years I have had clients, employees, vendors, suppliers, partners, and so forth of virtually every diversity segment. I have done business with those old and young, gay and straight, physically and mentally gifted, and physically and mentally challenged. I have worked with those that are in shape, out of shape, and of all races, creeds, and cultures. I have done business with the highly religious, the agnostic, and the atheist.

In each and every case my decisioning had nothing to do with diversity. My decisions had to do with the whole of the person and the best interests of the business.

My point is simply this: Smart leaders don't conduct business on the basis of diversity. They choose to do business based upon doing the right thing, rather than doing things right. They care about what is in the best interests of the business and those they serve more than what someone thinks about their employee mix. When it comes down to a hiring decision, good leaders simply don't care about your race, but they care greatly about whether you are the best person for the job. Good leaders will not promote you based on your ethnicity, gender, age, and so on, but they will promote you based upon your character and contribution.

The diversity argument is divisive and only serves to enable unqualified people to gain an advantage over those who are qualified. My advice is simple—don't identify yourself based on diversity segment; identify yourself by your accomplishments and your character.

Hacking Scalability

I've often said, "If leadership doesn't scale, neither will your organization." Experience has led me to conclude there is no greater contribution a leader can make to the enterprise than developing a true culture of leadership. Here's the thing—a culture of leadership can only exist when leaders understand their primary obligation is to develop other leaders. If leadership is sought after, valued, developed, and rewarded, then good things will happen.

Scale is not an individual endeavor—it's a cultural and organizational achievement that requires the right set of collaborative individual efforts. People don't scale, but effective groups, teams, and organizations can create scale. Well intended, but ill equipped leaders push individuals for more output, where savvy leaders teach and mentor individuals to think strategically and create leverage, which in turn, leads to scale.

There's a difference between acting strategically and understanding strategy. The most valuable leaders are not only astute, they're also insightful. They don't just think strategically; they shape strategy.

Perhaps most importantly, they ensure the sustainability of strategic focus by developing a culture of leadership.

Team members become most valuable to an organization when their strategic (thinking/teaching/mentoring/coaching) skills are leveraged far beyond what their tactical (doing) skills could ever achieve. When individuals enlighten, inform, and empower groups to be more productive, scale is achieved.

When individuals are pushed to simply "do more," both the quality and quantity of performance declines. The simple truth is most process glitches and production bottlenecks are individual choke points, not system errors. Scale is not a production issue, technology issue, or money issue—it's a leadership issue.

Great leaders view each interaction, question, or even conflict as a coaching opportunity. Don't answer questions or solve problems just because you can, rather teach your employees how to do it for themselves. If you make a habit of solving problems for people, you simply teach them to come to you for solutions at the first sign of a challenge.

So, how do you get your organization to create scale? Stop talking about process and start talking with your people. The following five steps will help you create a culture of leadership and create a scalable organization:

1. **Focus on Leadership:** Everything in business begins and ends with leadership. That said, leadership doesn't just exist at the top of an organization, but should be expected of everyone within the organization. Hire leaders, develop them to become better leaders, and teach them to repeat the process.

2. **Organization First:** Leadership is influencing the thoughts and actions of others so that individual interests are aligned with business interests. This becomes a reality when placing the organization ahead of the individual becomes culturally ingrained thinking. To truly understand the value of scalable leadership it's important to first understand the two primary causes of why leadership doesn't scale. When individual leaders, or even worse, leadership teams view themselves as the doers and not teachers, mentors, and coaches, organizational scale is quickly sacrificed on the altar of ego and/or incompetence.

3. **Do Away with Form over Substance:** I have grown to have a great distaste for 9 box thinking when it comes to leadership development. I question the best practice mentality of labeling people, and putting them in a box. If talent management and succession planning were as easy as identifying "high potentials," the business world would have many more success stories than currently exist. In fact, I would go so far as to say the phrases *key employee* or *high potential* are outdated, elitist terms that create angst and animosity among the ranks. Good leaders view all employees as key, and great leaders don't label people as high potentials—they ensure people achieve their potential. The fact companies single out someone as "key" or "high potential" to begin with means at a minimum they have a lack of transparency and continuity in their organizations, and more probably, they lack depth of talent and are weak in process and knowledge management.

4. **Drive Decision Rights Down:** The best organizations drive the most complex decisions down to the lowest possible levels within the company. If all big decisions are made by an individual, or a small group of individuals, your organization won't scale. Teach the organization and its employees how to make great decisions and then provide them with the authority to do so.

5. **Embrace Dissenting Opinion:** Conflict and challenge are part of change. If you stifle candor and free thought, you stifle the ability to scale. When leaders engage people with stimulating and probing conversation they learn and grow.

The take-away here is that great leaders don't create a state of dependency. In fact, they won't allow dependencies to exist—rather they mandate independent thinking and decision making. Many leaders struggle with understanding that rescuing is not the same thing as leading. To create a culture of leadership and a framework for scale, stop feeding your employees and teach them how to fish.

Hacking the Me Too Gap—Don't Copy, Create

I can't even begin to count the number of times I've witnessed companies try to copy another organization's culture rather than create their own. You'd be surprised at the number of leaders who would rather research and study other corporate cultures than simply ask their team what it will take to improve their own culture.

If you want to understand what's going on inside your organization, simply ask those who spend their waking hours as participants in the culture. Engage with those closest to the issues—not those furthest removed from them. Seek first the answers from within your organization not from without.

Probably the most common example of this flawed thinking can be found in companies that attempt to hire away employees of an "it" company like Google, Apple, Amazon, and so on, in hope they'll inject some magic into their enterprise. Really? If only the complexity of culture issues were as simple as raiding the employee ranks of another company. . . . Making the assumption hiring Apple or Google employees could universally solve the talent woes of other organizations is wishful thinking at best. Just ask J.C. Penney how the Ron Johnson experiment worked out for them.

The recent debacle with Ron Johnson and J.C. Penney is just another example of a board of directors tapping the wrong CEO for the job. Penney's opted for star power, when what they should have done was hire a CEO with proven turnaround experience. Penney's didn't need *cool*—they needed someone who understood the JCP culture, the JCP consumer, and the JCP business, all of which varied radically from Johnson's Apple experience.

Penney's board opted for a silver bullet that didn't exist. Rather than do the hard work and heavy lifting necessary to turn around a brand that had been mismanaged for years, they wanted a quick fix—they bought smoke and mirrors rather than sound business practice. You can't lead with cool—cool must be earned. The label of cool comes as a result of great business decisions and outstanding leadership.

While JCP was broken long before Johnson took the helm, the retailer's performance clearly declined under his leadership. The thing is, it didn't have to happen, and oddly enough, I blame Penney's board and their search firm just as much as Johnson. There were a dozen candidates who would have been a better selection, but they just had a demonstrable track of turning around businesses—they weren't considered *cool*. Here's the thing—had they made the right choice, for the right reasons, everyone would be looking cool right now. Succession matters—especially CEO successions.

Bottom line: You cannot short-cut the process of creating a culture of leadership by simply copying the aspects of another corporate culture. Create your own vision, stick to your values, hire employees who share your vision and values, do the hard work, and stay the course.

As I've alluded to in other places between the covers of the book, simply adopting someone else's best practices offer no assurances of similar outcomes. Success is created—not copied.

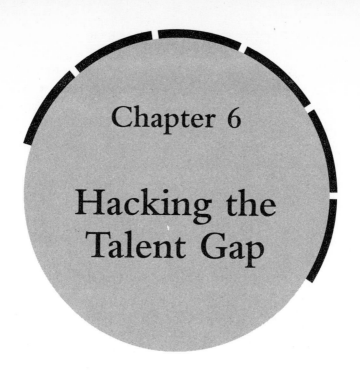

Chapter 6

Hacking the Talent Gap

Leaders don't put people in boxes; it's their obligation to free them from boxes. True leadership is about helping people reach places they didn't know they could go.

I t is one thing to be able to recruit talent, something altogether different to properly deploy talent, and quite another thing to have your talent play nicely in collaboration with one another. It is the responsibility of leadership to set the tone with a great talent strategy. Leaders who don't understand how to hack the talent gaps in their organization will find themselves at a continuous competitive disadvantage.

Hacking the Trust Gap

I can't think of a better way to begin a discussion on talent than to address the topic of trust. All the talent in the world won't overcome a

lack of trust and loyalty. Over the years I've heard the following statement on more than a few occasions: "I don't have to trust them, I just
have to work with them." My question is this; why would you want to
work with someone you cannot trust?

I never cease to be amazed at the great number of leaders who
believe they can operate effectively in the absence of trust. Let me
make this as clear as I can—you cannot build a culture of leadership
where trust is not valued, respected, and required.

My advice on trust is rather simple—if you have people on your
team you don't trust, find a way to develop trust or replace them—
there is no other prudent option. Trust is far too vital to the health of
an organization to be trivialized. Trust is not a commodity, and trust
is not something to be dismissed as useless or irrelevant. Trust is the
cornerstone of leadership. Without trust being both extended and
received, leaders, teams, and ultimately organizations will fail.

True wisdom is not fleeting, and therefore the proof of real wisdom is found in its ability to stand the test of time. The phrase "A
house divided against itself cannot stand" is most commonly referred
to as a quote from a speech given by Abraham Lincoln. However, the
statement dates back much further in time to words spoken by Jesus
in the Gospel of Mark. I make reference to this truism only to validate the importance of trust and alignment in the context of leadership and teamwork. Trust must be both implicitly and explicitly
present for leadership to be effective and for teams to thrive. As the
statement above proves, this concept has been known to be true for
centuries.

One of the things that must be addressed in any discussion on the
topic of trust is how blame is dealt with. Leadership today seems to
be all too often confused with playing a game of dodgeball. It's as if
many leaders show up for work each day with a freshly applied coat
of Teflon, ready to duck and dodge anything that comes their way. Let
me be clear—I appreciate savvy and finesse as much as the next person, but not as a substitute for courage. We have too many people in
leadership positions who either can't or won't accept responsibility for
anything. Put simply, leadership is about accountability, and not only
being willing to take the hit, but also being capable of surviving the hit.
Leadership *is* ownership.

If your immediate response to a problem is to spin, deflect, or blame-shift, then you've got a lot to learn about leadership. Those you lead are not looking for you to step back or step aside from issues; they're looking for you to step up and hit issues head on. The fastest way to lose respect as a leader is to focus on optics over ethics. If you're more concerned about political fallout than solving the problem, you have failed as a leader. Even though responsibility for decisions defaults to the leader, responsibility should be a thing of design, not default. It should be readily accepted and not easily denied—this is real leadership.

The entire world seems to be crying out for real leadership right now. Not leaders in title, but leaders in action. Whether in the boardroom, political arena, or on the frontlines leadership is far more than holding press conferences, giving speeches, and presiding over meetings and committees. Leadership can be boiled down into either owning the responsibility for getting things done or failing to do so. Remember, specificity of thought and deed shatters the comfort and safety sought by those who prefer to remain in the shadows of vague rhetoric.

Let's look at this another way—when was the last time you held a leader in high regard who dodged the issue, didn't do the right thing, failed to accept responsibility, took credit for another person's achievements, or blamed someone else for their mistakes? My guess is that your answer, as it should be, is never. While people will take issue with arrogance or ignorance, they will usually accept an honest mistake—especially where sincere contrition and remorse exist. But know this; few people will ever trust self-serving leadership.

Here's the thing—sane people don't expect perfection from leaders, but they do expect leaders to be transparent and accountable. Accepting responsibility for your actions, or the actions of your team, makes you honorable, and trustworthy—it also humanizes you. People don't want the talking head of a politician for a leader, they want someone they can connect to, and relate with. They not only want someone they trust, but someone who trusts them as well.

If you take one thing away from this it should be this: Leadership isn't about you, your ego, your pride, or your personal ambition—it's about caring for and serving those you lead, while accomplishing the mission at hand. Leadership has very little to do with the leader, and everything to do with those being led. I knew a great football coach who used to say, "Step up and take the hit, or get off the field." My sentiments exactly.

Time for a reality check, and here's where things get a little tougher—there are only a few certainties in life, and sadly, having the trust you've placed in someone be abused is one of them. Moreover, either intentionally or unintentionally we have all broken trust with others at some point in our lives. We know how it feels to be on both sides of the equation—betrayal hurts, it's not fair, it can create bitterness and resentment, it has huge ripple effects, it can rock your world.

All of this said, wise people learn from their own mistakes as well as the mistakes of others. They especially use the most tragic of circumstances as teachable moments and learning opportunities. The issue isn't whether or not you've made errors in judgment, or whether others have wronged you—we all have experienced both sides of this coin. The question is this: Are you capable of doing the right thing so that you can learn, grow, develop, bridge gaps, and move forward?

When it comes to the issue of broken trust there are really only three options: (1) repair it—understand why a breach occurred, find common ground, and gain/give assurances it won't happen again; (2) decide to live with a fractured relationship where trust is absent; or (3) decide to end the relationship. Leadership isn't about being right; it's about doing the right thing. Where this concept really gets put to the test is after *you* have made a mistake. I've always said the true test of leaders is what they do in the moments immediately after they realize they are wrong.

We need to keep in mind that all people make mistakes, and that mistakes alone don't necessarily make you evil, they just make you human. That said, human nature is to be much quicker with forgiving ourselves than forgiving others. I'm not suggesting leaders should forgive all mistakes, but if leaders forgive no mistakes, then people will cease taking risks, they won't give their real opinions, and eventually they'll stop making decisions. Be a leader who leads—not one who governs by creating a culture of fear.

I recently had the chance to speak with Mother Teresa's former interpreter. It was one of the most pleasurable hours of conversation I've spent in quite some time. This man has seen his fair share of hard times, burden and tragedy. Nonetheless, I was in awe of his compassion, empathy, and sense of justice. It was as if I was looking into the soul of Mother Teresa through the lens of this man's experiences. It reminded me of something Mother Teresa once said:

> People are often unreasonable and self-centered.
> *Forgive them anyway.*
>
> If you are kind, people may accuse you of ulterior motives.
> *Be kind anyway.*
>
> If you are honest, people may cheat you.
> *Be honest anyway.*
>
> If you find happiness, people may be jealous.
> *Be happy anyway.*
>
> The good you do today may be forgotten tomorrow.
> *Do good anyway.*
>
> Give the world the best you have, and it may never be enough.
> *Give your best anyway.*
>
> For you see, in the end, it is between you and God.
> *It was never between you and them anyway.*

While it is much easier to avoid disaster than it is to recover from it, perhaps the most important lesson is that it's not the mistake you make, but what you do with your life after the fact—will your mistakes define you as a failure and disgrace, or will they serve as the impetus to correct your thinking and actions such that you redefine yourself to become a better and more trustworthy human being? Don't fear mistakes—fear not having the courage to make them. Leaders should be far more concerned with being wrong than they are being proven wrong.

Hacking the Loyalty Gap

It's virtually impossible to discuss trust without tying it to loyalty. Keeping this in mind: Is it just me, or has loyalty become rather scarce these days? Anyone who's been in leadership for any length of time has likely pulled more than a few knives out of their back. Bottom line—there seems to be way too much focus on *me* and not enough focus on *we* these days.

There have always been those who have fostered trust and earned loyalty, as well as those who have abused both for personal gain. But in this "what have you done lately for me" society where relationships have degenerated into little more than stepping stones, loyalty seems to be elusive at best. One of a leader's most important functions is to create an environment where trust and loyalty are the rule and not the exception.

If relationships are the currency of leadership, it is important for leaders to note that loyalty serves as the cornerstone of any healthy relationship. Leadership and loyalty go hand in hand. In fact, so much so that leaders who fail to understand this simply won't endure the test of time. While successful leaders share many common traits, all great leaders understand this: They are not only adept at earning the loyalty of those they lead, but they also recognize that loyalty is a two-way street. When it comes to loyalty, the simple rule is that you will not receive what you will not give.

I think it's important for leaders to do a gut check and take note of the difference between fear-based loyalty and trust-based loyalty. As a leader, do you command the loyalty of those around you because of your title, or have you earned it by gaining their trust and respect?

Loyalty commanded is fleeting; loyalty earned is enduring. **Hint—** to be feared as a leader is not a badge of honor to be sought after. It's one thing for employees to have a healthy respect for you, but quite another to be in fear of you. Remember that respect is earned, and fear is imposed. Fear-based motivations don't instill loyalty, create trust, build morale, inspire creativity, attract talent, or drive innovation. The truth is that fear stifles, and if left unchecked, eventually kills all of the aforementioned attributes.

If you're a leader who has created a fear-based culture I can guarantee you two things: (1) your employees won't give you their best, and (2) when things get tough, or other opportunities present themselves, your employees will cut and run at the first option that comes their way because you have failed to earn their loyalty. As a leader, if you believe that instilling fear in your employees is a good thing, you may be a tyrannical bully, but you are certainly not an effective leader.

Remember that great leaders see themselves *not* as masters of the universe, but as inspirational servants, catalysts, teachers, and team builders. Again, I would strongly encourage you to think "leader" and not "dictator." Reflect back to your time as a student. Which educators brought out the best in you? My guess is that it was not the *know it all* professors who lived to put you in your place and show you how much they knew and you didn't. My suspicion is your best memories are of those teachers who inspired you, encouraged you, brought out your passion, and challenged you in a positive fashion. I would also suspect you produced your best work for the latter and not the former.

So, how do you tell if your employees respect you or fear you? After reading the above comments it should already be obvious, but just in case, review the five items below:

1. **A Team of Yes-Men:** Feared leaders either surround themselves with like-minded people or train people to share their views in a vacuum. Either way they lose. Great leaders value the opinions of their team, whether or not these views happen to be in concurrence with their own beliefs. The best leaders not only subject their ideas to scrutiny—they openly encourage it.

2. **Lack of Interaction:** Along the lines of number one above, if executives, management, and staff don't proactively seek your advice and input, then you have a respect problem. They either don't value your contributions, or they know from experience that you'll treat their inquiry in a belittling fashion. Over time, many fear-based leaders unknowingly train their team to think: "Why even try if there is no upside? The boss will never go for that."

3. **Lack of Feedback:** If as a leader you don't subject yourself to a 360 review process, then you are not earnestly looking for personal growth and development opportunities. Here's an ego check—if you do utilize a 360 review, and all the responses are positive, evaluate whether this has occurred because you are feared and are thus the recipient of insincere flattery, or because you have the loyalty and respect of those you lead.

4. **Revolving Door:** If you either can't attract or retain tier-one talent, you are not an effective leader who has earned the respect and loyalty of your team. In fact, upon closer examination, you'll find

that you probably don't have a team. Sad but true, real talent won't be attracted to, or remain engaged with, leaders who operate on fear-based tactics.

5. **Poor Performance:** Leaders who have the respect of their team will outperform those that don't. Leaders who attempt to use command and control tactics without the necessary underpinnings of real leadership principles will simply not do well. If your organization is not thriving and growing, then the first thing that should occur is a long look in the mirror. Begin your triage by first evaluating your leadership qualities or the lack thereof.

Ask yourself the following question: If your employees held an election today, would you be reelected to your current position by a landslide, or would you be voted out? Bottom line—what is rightfully earned and freely given (loyalty, trust, and respect) will always outlast what is imprudently acquired for the wrong reasons (the bully tactics of fear-based control). For me it's an easy call—you stand by those you trust and respect, and you don't abandon them because it's popular or convenient. Loyalty matters.

Hacking the Four Dimensions of Talent

I tend to look at talent from a four-dimensional perspective: First Dimension—what you were born with; Second Dimension—what you do with what you're born with; Third Dimension—to what extent you develop beyond your natural abilities and giftedness; and Fourth Dimension—how you develop and scale talent in others.

Great leaders maximize opportunities across all four dimensions, while less accomplished leaders try to leverage one or two dimensions. The simple truth of the matter is that one- and two-dimensional leaders simply cannot accomplish what three- and four-dimensional leaders can.

Many of you are familiar with what's commonly referred to as the *great man theory* and/or the debate surrounding the born versus made argument. These conversations have been floating around leadership circles since the dawn of time. While I find this topic somewhat sophomoric, it nonetheless deserves a bit of airtime to clear up any misunderstandings or flaws in logic.

So, are leaders born or made? While there is a very simple answer to this question, most people are so entrenched in their beliefs that no amount of reason or logic will alter their opinions. But, hey, that's never stopped me before. . . . For my part, I would actually like to make an attempt at putting this useless debate to bed once and for all.

So, what's the answer? *Both*—some people are born with innate qualities that predispose them to being leaders, and other people, while not naturally gifted with leadership ability, can acquire it. Moreover, all leaders, born or made, can improve their ability with desire, experience, and effort.

If we're to be honest with ourselves, as opposed to defending a particular position to suit our needs, we've all known born leaders. They are those affable individuals who possess charisma and presence, combined with the ability to make good decisions—people have flocked to them since an early age. They were your class presidents, team captains, club leaders, and the people who held virtually all the available leadership positions you can imagine early in life. They were those unflappable individuals who seemed to just have that "it" factor. They were the born leaders we all grew up with.

Before we move on, and as a caution to those naturally gifted leaders, natural ability will only take you so far. Leaders comfortable resting on their laurels, without making the effort to develop their skills, will eventually be overtaken by those who view leadership as a professional skill to be developed and refined. As the old saying goes, " It's not what you've been given, but what you do with it that matters." People have to decide for themselves whether they'll be underachievers or people who excel, and since you'll be judged for your choice, my suggestion would be to choose wisely.

Moving on, we've all also known individuals who while perhaps not naturally gifted leaders, either fell into or accepted leadership responsibility, and worked diligently to develop themselves into highly effective leaders. Leadership acumen can most certainly be taught, and it can also be ingrained in those willing to put forth the effort to learn.

You see, the only thing that keeps someone from becoming a sound leader is a lack of character, effort, and desire. If those three qualities are present, everything else can be developed. I've personally witnessed the shy and introverted develop presence, the greedy become giving, the arrogant develop an authentic sense of humility, the foolish become discerning and wise, people who struggled with decision making learn solid decisioning skills, individuals who lacked domain expertise acquire it, people who were ego centric transition into servant leaders, and the list could go on . . .

Bottom line: It is not how leaders come by their skill that is relevant. It only matters that they possess the requisite skills for the job, and that they are willing to apply those skills for the benefit of those they lead. Remember, there is no perfect leader, no single right way to lead, and no one-size-fits-all formula for leadership. Let's stop wasting time debating whether leaders are born or made, and focus on how to help them be better leaders regardless of how they arrived.

Let's delve a bit deeper into the "what you were born with" issue. While not all leaders will develop their talents and abilities to the same level, all successful leaders more or less begin with the same foundation. Clearly the difference possessed by all great leaders is that they refine, develop, and build from their foundation—they don't ignore it or take it for granted. As much as some don't want to admit it, the foundational elements of leadership require no skill or talent whatsoever.

What we're experiencing today is too much form over substance—leaders lacking in foundation, but replete with social/political savvy. You can work with someone where the basics are in place, but lacking certain fundamentals, there really isn't much you can do. Organizations would be well served to move past the infatuation with beauty contests and look for real strength in the areas that matter. In the list that follows I'm going to share with you six leadership characteristics that require absolutely no talent or ability, but that must be present in order to succeed over the long haul as a leader.

1. **Show Up:** You can't make a difference if you don't show up. It requires zero talent to be present mentally and physically. In most sports I'm aware of, you cannot play if you don't suit up and show up. Leadership is a participation sport and never works well in absentia.

2. **Care:** There is great truth in the old axiom "people don't care how much you know until they know how much you care." Extending basic human courtesy requires no talent—just a willingness to behave in a decent manner. It's highly probable that you don't like rude, elitist, arrogant, dismissive, or condescending people, so don't become one yourself.

3. **Hustle:** I learned this lesson at an early age. I had a basketball coach take me aside after I finished far ahead of the pack after a long set of down-and-backs. He pointed to a slower teammate who was still running his lines and said, "He may not be as fast, but he's giving 100 percent—Did you?" He went on to say, "It takes no talent to hustle, and your team deserves better." I don't ever remember dogging it again.

4. **Follow Through:** It takes no ability to simply do what you say you're going to do. Nothing is more important for a leader than keeping promises and commitments. A leader who fails to understand this will never create the trust bond necessary to lead effectively. It's just not that hard to deliver on your promises, and if you have no intention of doing so, don't make the commitment to begin with.

5. **Positive Attitude:** To the one, the best leaders I've ever known all smile, listen, engage, have a positive outlook, and have a high energy level. This is a mind-set thing, not a talent thing—it's as simple as making the choice to be pleasant.

6. **Do the Right Thing:** While it will often require courage, it takes no talent or ability to recognize the difference between right and wrong. Real leaders don't compromise when it comes to core values. It takes no skill to tell the truth, and great leaders will always forgo doing things right where such actions conflict with doing the right thing.

There is no doubt that the list above could be expanded. There are large numbers of leadership characteristics that require no talent or ability, just desire.

Hacking the Hiring Gap

Do you ever find yourself wondering how so many good companies can make so many bad hires? The fact is, all the rigorous and sophisticated hiring processes employed by the best companies in the world don't prevent bad hires. The good news is, addressing one single factor can easily prevent the majority of bad hires.

When companies view hiring as a process instead of an art form, the masterpiece they seek will certainly be lost in mass production. Think about talent acquisition more from a design thinking perspective than a systems thinking perspective. The latter will filter for average talent, while the former will attract great talent.

The number-one reason companies make bad hires is they compromise, they settle, they don't hire the *best person* for the job. Compromise has its place in business, but it has no role in the acquisition of talent. Leaders too often focus on the "nice to haves" instead of the "must haves." They allow themselves to be distracted by disparate, insignificant factors, rather than holding out for the best person for the job.

As I've noted before, my definition of irony: when leaders complain about their talent. I've always believed leaders deserve the teams they build. Here's the thing—when leaders make a bad hire they have no one to blame but themselves. The problem is many leaders place the blame everywhere but where it belongs.

It doesn't matter whether candidates have great potential, what diversity segment they represent, if the hire is an internal or external candidate, whether or not they have industry experience, or where they earned their degree. What matters is whether they are the *best* person for the job. Smart leaders don't "give" people the job because they've been with the company longer—they select the best person for the job regardless of how long they've been with the company.

How many times have you witnessed a company lose their preferred candidate over a trivial point of difference, and then have the company only proceed to compound their problem by settling for their second or even third choice? Smart leaders understand an open position is preferable to filling a position with the wrong candidate.

There is truth in the old axiom "talent begets talent." Talent is a contagion. It's talent that fuels creativity, collaboration, momentum, velocity, client loyalty, a dynamic corporate culture, and virtually every other positive influencing force in the corporate universe. It's talent that designs sound business practices, develops strategic plans, understands the value of innovation, overcomes obstacles, breaks down barriers, creates growth, and builds a lasting brand. Smart leaders hire only the best person for the job. They don't compromise on talent.

Good enough rarely is, and just checking the box is not the business of leadership. While it's required to evaluate hard skills, track record, leadership ability, cultural fit, and any number of other criteria, it's completely irresponsible to settle for anything less than the best person for the job. Don't allow yourself to be bounded by time frames, compensation guidelines, or pressure from individuals or key constituencies—hold out for the best people, and when you find them, move heaven and earth to hire them.

Aside from what we just discussed above, I've noticed that many in the business of talent acquisition simply overlook the obvious. In other words, the people doing the hiring fail to understand, look for, and qualify the one characteristic that indicates the certainty of a good hire. While companies screen for many things, they often miss the gold standard litmus test—they play a game of chance when it's simply not necessary.

I can remember just casually reading the results of a recent survey on the topic of hiring methodologies when one particular survey question jumped off the page at me: "When considering a new hire, what is the one characteristic or attribute of the candidate that would most influence your hiring decision?" The "right" answer seemed quite obvious to me, but in reading the respondents' (100 hiring managers, executives, and HR types) answers, I was truly amazed at what I saw. . . . It's no wonder companies make bad hires when they make decisions based on the *wrong* evaluation metrics.

Let me begin by sharing some of the representative answers (not mine) that were put forth in response to the survey question above:

- "Leadership ability" (a very good answer but not the right one)
- "I would have to say being a good communicator"
- "The ability to think outside the box and eagerness to learn"
- "The ability to make a good first impression"
- "Intelligence"
- "Passion"
- "Commitment to invest long hours"
- "Being a team player"

- "Excellent time management skills"
- "Enthusiastic attitude"
- "Strong analytical abilities"
- "Solid technical skills"
- "The ability to execute"
- "The ability to follow process"
- "That the individual is a nice person"
- "That they have a degree from a good school"

Did you notice anything missing from the list? Again, keep in mind these (along with the other answers posted) were given by senior managers and executives. Here's what I'd like you to consider: While the answers noted above all point to admirable traits, when you evaluate them based upon the context of the original question posed, they are woefully inadequate, and nothing short of mystifying. Out of 100 answers provided *only two* respondents answered with what I believe is the correct answer: "Integrity and Character."

You see, any of the traits identified in the 98 other answers absent character and integrity will eventually lead to some type of disconnect or debacle. Put another way, if you can't trust people to do the right thing, it doesn't matter how likable, passionate, or talented they are. You can teach many things, but altering the hardwiring of an adult's character is best left to a therapist or the clergy—not an employer.

A values-based approach to hiring increases performance, enhances collaboration, reduces turnover, improves morale, and creates a stable culture. The fact that character and integrity showed as poorly as they did in the survey is proof positive for why the corporate workplace struggles with hiring. If you're going to probe for something, probe for character.

What should be jumping off the page here is that based upon the above referenced survey only 2 percent of the companies surveyed appear to utilize a values-based hiring methodology. Moreover, one might conclude that 98 percent of these companies have the wrong people doing the hiring. I strongly suggest that whoever is doing the hiring within your organization utilize a values-based recruiting model.

This doesn't just mean hire a top producer, or the candidate who graduated from the best business school, but rather hire a quality individual who is a person of integrity and character. A person whose values are in alignment with the organizations core values and vision, and who also happens to be talented.

The simple truth of the matter is you can have your cake and eat it too, if you're willing to hold out for the right person. It simply isn't necessary to compromise on core values to acquire talent. New hires should desire to be part of your company for more than the ability to maximize immediate earning potential—they should be interested in your company because there is a sincere alignment of values and vision. My premise is a simple one—there is no talent shortage, just a shortage of those able to recognize it.

Don't be quick to hire based upon gut feel, but rather take time in the interviewing process to let the prospective new hire get a feel for your culture and your company. Never oversell the company, but rather disclose all the problems and weaknesses of the organization so the candidate can make a good decision that won't later be unwound by inconsistent messaging or practices. Above all, don't be seduced by qualities that while they may be attractive on the surface, won't ever make up for a lack of character and integrity.

Hacking the Definition Gap

I've always believed leaders must know what they're looking for in order to find it. So let me ask you this—When was the last time you read a leadership job description? We have job descriptions for every position under the sun, but I've yet to see one for leaders. Virtually every job description you'll read lists "leadership ability" as a quality/characteristic/attribute that is valued, and in fact, most list it as a requirement. So why is it we place so much value in leaders, when we can't even define leadership? It's critically important to understand the role of a leader *before* you place someone in a leadership role.

Every major corporation on the face of the planet has a leadership development program, but I challenge you to find a definition of leadership anywhere in the curriculum. I find it nothing short of astonishing that billions of dollars are spent each year on leadership training, leadership development, leadership coaching, running high-potential programs, and so forth when the companies and individuals implementing these initiatives can't even tell you what they're trying to achieve. Here's the thing—how do you hire, train, and develop to a standard that doesn't exist?

In the absence of a clear definition for leadership, the reality is that many of today's leaders are suffering from an identity crisis. The magnitude of this crisis can range from a distorted, diluted, destructive, and in some cases deranged form of what people inaccurately define as leadership when not held to a clearly articulated, well-defined standard. Because those in leadership roles have failed to define leadership in an acceptable fashion, society has allowed the practice of leadership to be commoditized, which in turn, has made it all too common for non-leaders to assume leadership positions thus continuing the devolution of leadership as a practice.

When we devalue the worth of leadership, it only follows that many people will in turn devalue their worth as a leader. Many leaders today simply do not understand what leadership is, which is precisely why we find ourselves in a crisis of leadership. I would suggest much of what we view today being represented as leadership is actually unleadership—a cheap imitation of the real thing by those who are role-playing, but clearly are not leading.

When leaders become lost and confused, it doesn't just impact them—it creates a ripple effect through an organization with a destructive force much more closely resembling a tsunami. Leadership isn't about maximizing a W-2, and it's not about personal glory or media attention. Put simply, true leadership isn't about the leader.

Leadership is more than a title; it's a privilege and therefore a burden of the highest responsibility. Nothing is more dangerous than leaders who lose sight of their real purpose—to serve something greater than themselves. Leadership is about qualities that recognize others while bringing out the best in them. Leadership cannot flourish with small minds, thinking about small things, in small ways.

In thinking about the countless discussions I've participated in on the topic of leadership, I noticed an interesting paradox: While many of you vehemently disagree on the effectiveness (or lack thereof) of different leadership styles, most of you are in total agreement on the qualities and attributes possessed by great leaders regardless of style.

In further pondering this dichotomy an interesting thought came to mind: If I could genetically engineer the perfect leadership gene, what qualities and characteristics would constitute the architecture of leadership DNA?

So, what traits/qualities/characteristics would my perfect leader possess? Courage, character, humility, vision, wisdom, integrity, empathy, persistence, compassion, aggressivity, discernment, commitment, confidence, a bias to action, the ability to resolve conflict, a servant's heart, determination, creativity, self-discipline, love, loyalty, outstanding decision-making ability, engaged, authentic, transparent, a great strategic thinker, passion, a positive attitude, intelligence, great communication skills, common sense, generosity, the ability to identify and develop great talent, someone who creates a certainty of execution, attention to detail, faith, an active listener, a prolific learner, respect for others, innovative, excellent tactical capability, charisma, extreme focus, a high risk tolerance, a broad range of competencies, and the list goes on. . . .

If any of you possess all the above attributes please forward your resume to my attention! All kidding aside, the longer my list of desirable qualities became, the more I realized the frivolity of this exercise: *There is no perfect leader; only the right leader for a given situation.* Great leaders have the innate ability to call on the right skills in a contextually and environmentally appropriate fashion. No single leader can possess every needed attribute. It's not the traits you possess as a leader, but what you do with them that matters. If I were successful in my genetic engineering exercise, I would no doubt have created a leader who would be driven crazy by emotional and intellectual conflicts.

So, what is real leadership? Leadership is about giving credit not taking it, breaking down barriers not building them, destroying bureaucracies not creating them, bridging positional and philosophical gaps not setting boundaries, thinking big and acting bigger, being able to focus on short-term objectives without losing sight of long-term value, not focusing on the volume of outputs but the impact of those outputs, surrender not control, and most of all, leadership is about truly caring for those whom you serve.

Since I've admonished those who have failed to define leadership, let me put forth my definition for your consideration—while it's a bit wordy, I've found it to inclusively articulate the principles needed for effective leadership:

> Leadership is the professed desire and commitment to serve others by subordinating personal interests to the needs of those being led through effectively demonstrating the character, experience, humility, wisdom, and discernment necessary to create the trust and influence to cause the right things, to happen for the right reasons, at the right times.

My challenge to those "playing leadership" is to abandon the practice of unleadership. I encourage you to stop contributing to the crisis of leadership and instead begin contributing to a culture of leadership. Define leadership, hold leaders to a standard, build into others, don't tolerate the status quo, and inspire greatness. When it comes to leadership, it's not enough to be all you can be, you must focus on helping others become all that they can be.

Hacking the Quality Gap—Supply versus Demand

In the previous chapter, we talked a lot about culture. While it should be obvious to all, the first step in cultural design is to be very, very careful whom you let through the front door. People, their traits, attitudes, and work ethic (or lack thereof) are contagions. This can be positive or negative—the choice is yours. The old saying, "talent begets talent," is true, but talent that aligns with culture will produce better results than talent that does not.

Great leaders surround themselves with great talent. They understand that talent begets talent. There's an old saying that A talent attracts $A+$ talent, while B talent attracts C talent. There has never been a truer statement. If your company doesn't possess the talent it needs to achieve its business objectives, no one is to blame but leadership.

The first talent hack all leaders must learn is perhaps the most obvious one, but you'd be surprised at the number of people in leadership roles who miss it altogether. Talent Hack #1: Don't be a jerk. There is great truth in the old axiom "people don't care how much you know until they know how much you care." Extending basic human courtesy requires no skill—just a willingness to behave in a decent manner. It's highly probable that you don't like rude, elitist, arrogant, dismissive, or condescending people, so don't become one yourself.

To the one, the best leaders I've ever known all smile, listen, engage, have a positive outlook, and have a high energy level. This is a mind-set thing, not a competency thing—it's as simple as making the choice to be pleasant.

Hacking the Consensus Gap

One of the things I've witnessed leaders struggle with is their desire to be "fair" in all their dealings. While a nice sentiment, and a politically correct one to be sure, it's simply not good leadership. The practice of leadership has little to do with being fair, and everything to do with achieving the right outcome. I'm not recommending a means to an end approach to leadership, but rather replacing the thought of being fair, with that of being just—they are not one in the same.

The problem with a fairness doctrine approach is it leads to a groupthink mentality, which then leads to consensus thinking. The problem with consensus thinking is most people don't understand its danger. While all people may be created equal, they are certainly *not* all equals in the workplace.

The thought that all employees should have an equal say might be an idealistic thought, but it's not practical, nor is it productive. While I'm a true believer in candor in the workplace, and have always encouraged feedback and input at every level of an organization, this doesn't mean everyone should have an equal say—they shouldn't.

Team building is not about equality at all—it has nothing to do with consensus. Rather team building is about alignment of vision with expectations, ensuring team members clearly understand their roles, and making sure they have the right resources to perform their duties with exacting precision. Consensus thinking is devastating to all things productive.

I've often said that theory without action amounts to little more than useless rhetoric, and while most companies are spinning their wheels pontificating on the merits of team building, it is the truly great organizations that put theory into practice. Great leaders intrinsically understand that team building catalyzes collaboration, creates both disruptive and incremental innovation, facilitates a certainty of execution, and is one of the key foundational elements associated with creating a dynamic corporate culture. Consensus thinking undermines all of the aforementioned. Consensus is team building's worst enemy; it is also often a great adversary of a healthy culture.

It is the responsibility of executive leadership to set the tone for great teamwork by putting forth a clearly articulated vision, and then aligning every aspect of strategic and tactical decisioning with said vision. A lack of clarity, obviously flawed business logic, or constantly shifting priorities/positions are the death of many a venture. However leaders who implement a well-thought-out and clearly articulated vision, create a sense of stability and a bond of trust among the ranks. This in turn leads to a very focused, coordinated, and, ultimately, a very passionate work environment. It is not too difficult to get your crew all oaring together when these characteristics are firmly in place because they now know which direction to row.

Team building should have nothing to do with ego, tenure, or titles, but rather it should be all about competency, collaboration, and productivity. Leaders must clearly communicate to team members what their duties, roles, and responsibilities are, as well as setting forth a road map for performance expectations. Team building, group dynamics, talent management, leadership development, and any number of other functional areas are much more about clarity, focus, aligning expectations, and defining roles than creating equality. If you examine the most effective teams in the real world you'll find numerous examples that support the thoughts being espoused in this text.

Whether you look at athletic teams, military teams, executive teams, management teams, technical teams, design teams, functional teams, or any other team, you'll find the best of the best have a few things in common. They value structure; a hierarchy of leadership; a clear understanding of roles, responsibilities, and expectations; clear and open lines of communication; and a well established decisioning protocol. But nowhere is equality found as a key success metric for teams.

Can you imagine the manager of a Major League Baseball team letting the players determine how the line-up card will be filled out? How about a drill sergeant letting recruits determine their own training regimen? Sadly, this is the type of thinking that has invaded far too many organizations. Making decisions by consensus usually result in no decision being made, or an intellectually dishonest, watered-down decision that is so full of compromises, hedges, and caveats that a non-decision might have been preferable.

Groupthink is a very dangerous practice. It stifles innovation, discourages candor, disdains dissenting opinions, and mutes the truth. If what you seek is to neutralize your advantage by dumbing down the insights, observations, and contributions of your team, then by all means default to consensus thinking.

Perhaps the greatest problem with consensus thinking is it stifles individual thought and contribution. As much as some don't want to hear this, there *is* an "I" in team—there is simply no getting around the fact that teams are comprised of individuals. If you crush the individual character and spirit of those who form your team, how can your team operate at its best? It cannot.

The strongest teams don't weed out, nor do they neutralize individual tendencies—they capitalize on them. The goal of leaders is *not* to clone themselves, but to harness individual strengths for the greater good of the team, and for the overall benefit of the organization. This is best accomplished by leveraging individual talents, not silencing them.

The simple fact is that no team can maximize its potential by ignoring or minimizing the strengths of individual members. While smart leaders seek to align expectations and to create unity in vision, they understand this has nothing to do with demanding conformity in thought, or perspective. In fact, savvy leaders do everything possible to inspire nonconformity in approach. It's only by stretching the boundaries of "normal" that organizations can fuel change and innovation.

If unique perspectives, philosophical differences, and dissenting opinions are viewed as an *opportunity* as opposed to a *setback*, growth and development are certain to follow. What I like to refer as "positional gaps" are best closed by listening to all sides, finding common ground, and then letting the principle of doing the right thing guide the process. When leaders develop the skill to transform negative conflict into creative tension, they have found the secret sauce for developing high performance teams. Mature leaders see individual differences as fuel for development, not as barriers to success.

It is absolutely possible to build very productive relationships with even the most adversarial of individuals. Regardless of a person's original intent, opinion, or position, the key to closing a positional gap is simply a matter of finding common ground in order to establish rapport. Moreover, building rapport is easily achieved assuming your motivations for doing so are sincere. I have always found that rapport is quickly developed when you listen, care, and attempt to help people succeed. By way of contrast, it is difficult to build rapport if you are driven by an agenda the other party sees as being a threat to its success or security.

While building and maintaining rapport with people whom you disagree with is certainly more challenging, many of the same rules expressed in my comments above still apply. I have found that often times dealing with difficult people simply just requires more intense focus on understanding the needs, wants, and desires of the other party. If opposing views are worth the time and energy to debate, then they are worth a legitimate effort to gain alignment on perspective, and resolution on position. However, this will rarely happen if lines of communication do not remain open. Candid, effective communication is best maintained through a mutual respect and rapport.

In an attempt to resolve conflicts, misunderstandings, or positional and/or philosophical gaps, the first step is to identify and isolate the specific areas of difference causing the difficulty. The sad fact is that many people in leadership positions are absolutists in that they only see things in terms of rights and wrongs. Thinking in terms of *my way* is right and therefore *other ways* are wrong is the basis for polarizing any relationship, which quickly results in converting discussions into power struggles. However, when a situation can be seen through the lens of difference, and a position is simply a matter of opinion not a totalitarian statement of fact, then collaboration is not only possible, it's probable. Identifying and understanding differences allows people (regardless of title) to evolve their thinking through rational and reasoned dialog. The following perspectives if kept top of mind will help in identifying and bridging positional gaps:

- Listening leads to understanding.
- Respect allows differences to evolve thought and create new behaviors.
- Accepting a person where they are creates a bond of trust.
- Trust, leads to a willingness to be open to:
  - New opportunities
  - New collaborations
  - New strategies
  - New ideas
  - New attitudes

The key to maximizing the individual talents within a team is to focus on the shared vision rather than individual differences. By adhering to the following eight principles, most individual points of departure can be used as a springboard for growth and innovation rather than a barrier:

1. **Be Consistent:** If your desire is to minimize misunderstandings, then I would suggest you stop confusing people. Say what you mean, mean what you say, and follow through on your commitments. Most people don't have to agree with you 100 percent of the time, but they do need to trust you 100 percent of the time. Trust cannot exist where leaders are fickle, inconsistent, indecisive, or display a lack of character. Never be swayed by consensus that calls you to compromise your values, rather be guided by doing the right thing. Finally, know that no person is universally right or universally liked, and become at peace with that.

2. **The Importance Factor:** Not every difference needs to be resolved. In fact, most differences don't require intervention as they actually contribute to a dynamic, creative, innovative culture. Remember that it's not important be right, and more importantly, that *you* don't have to be right for the right things to be accomplished. Pick your battles and avoid conflict for the sake of conflict. However, if the issue is important enough to create a conflict, then it is surely important enough to resolve. If the issue, circumstance, or situation is important enough, and there is enough at stake, people will do what is necessary to open lines of communication and close positional gaps.

3. **Make Respect a Priority:** Disagreement and disrespect are two different things, or at least they should be. Regardless of whether

or not perspectives and opinions differ, a position of respect should be adhered to and maintained. Respect is at the core of building meaningful relationships. It is the foundation that supports high performance teams, partnerships, superior and subordinate relationships, and peer-to-peer relationships. Respecting the right to differ while being productive is a concept that all successful executives and entrepreneurs master.

4. **Define Acceptable Behavior:** You know what they say about assuming. . . . Just having a definition for what constitutes acceptable behavior is a positive step in avoiding unnecessary conflict. Creating a framework for decisioning, using a published delegation of authority statement, encouraging sound business practices in collaboration, team building, leadership development, and talent management will all help avoid conflicts.

5. **Hit Conflict Head-On:** You can only resolve problems by proactively seeking to do so. While you can't always prevent conflicts, it has been my experience that the secret to conflict resolution is in fact conflict prevention where possible. By actually seeking out areas of potential conflict and proactively intervening in a well reasoned and decisive fashion you will likely prevent certain conflicts from ever arising. If a conflict does flair up, you will likely minimize its severity by dealing with it quickly.

6. **Understanding the WIIFM Factor:** Understanding the other person's WIIFM (What's In It For Me) position is critical. It is absolutely essential to understand others' motivations prior to weighing in. The way to avoid conflict is to help those around you achieve their objectives. If you approach conflict from the perspective of taking the action that will help others best achieve their goals, you will find that few obstacles will stand in your way with regard to resolving conflict.

7. **View Conflict as Opportunity:** Hidden within virtually every conflict is the potential for a tremendous teaching/learning opportunity. Where there is disagreement there is an inherent potential for growth and development. If you're a CEO who doesn't leverage conflict for team building and leadership development purposes, you're missing a great opportunity.

8. **Clarity of Purpose:** All the people who work for me know that I care about them as individuals. They are important to me. They

know that I'll go to great lengths to work with them so long as one thing remains the focus point—the good of the organization. So long as the issues being worked on are leading us toward our vision, they know they'll have my attention regardless of positional gaps or personal differences. Likewise, if things degenerate into placing pride or ego ahead of other team members or the organization as a whole, they know I'll have no tolerance whatsoever.

As I've already pointed out, people matter; but for people, organizations don't exist. It's often been said that a manager exists when the company says so, but that said manager only really becomes a leader when their team says so. As a leader, you have only two choices when it comes to your people—serve them and care for them. Sometimes this means working through challenging scenarios and situations. Leaders not up to this task should rethink their decision to lead.

"There is no 'I' in Team" and many other statements to that effect were never meant as endorsements for management by consensus. They are simply meant to foster a spirit of cooperation. Understanding how to lead and motivate groups and teams should not be considered one and the same with creating false perceptions of equality that don't exist. Real leadership means knowing when you should make the decision and when you should let others make the decision. Smart leaders may choose from time to time to give away authority, but they never give away responsibility—ultimately they own the decision regardless of who makes it and/or how it's made.

Bottom Line: Show me any team created of equals and I'll show you a team that will never reach its full potential. . . .

Hacking the One-Size-Doesn't-Fit-All Gap

Here's the thing—just because someone has succeeded in a particular role or at another organization doesn't mean they'll realize the same success in other endeavors. Likewise, just because someone has failed in a previous position doesn't mean they might not end up being a top performer in another company. Sure, other companies have some great talent, but it's talent identified, recruited, hired, and developed for the vision and culture of that organization, which may not be at all compatible with those of a different organization.

What makes the talent machine so impressive at "it" companies like Tesla, Apple, Google, Zappos, and others is they understand something many other organizations often talk about, but fail to grasp—it simply isn't necessary to compromise on core values to acquire great talent. That said, place an Apple employee in an organization with differing beliefs and ideals, a different set of core values, and a vision for the future that radically varies from their own, and I'd suggest said employee, albeit a talented employee, won't have the same impact on the new organization they had at Apple.

You can either spend time finding employees who share your organization's values and vision, or deal with the brain damage of managing conflicts that arise as a result of misalignment in these areas. A new hire should desire to be part of your company for more than the ability to maximize immediate earning potential—new hires should be interested in your company because there is a sincere alignment of values and vision. Trust me when I tell you that compromises in this area, which may seem insignificant during the interview process, will become visibly and materially significant down the road.

Hacking the Pressure Gap

I've always believed that talent thrives on pressure. How leaders deal with pressure will tell you much about who they are as people. Their reaction to pressure will reveal the strength of their character and conviction, what and whom they value, and whether or not they can be trusted. The reality is most people buckle under pressure. Only a few handle pressure well, and even fewer possess the qualities to be able to thrive on pressure.

There's no escaping pressure. And just in case you're wondering, denying its presence doesn't mean it doesn't exist, and won't make it go away. It's not a matter of *if* you'll encounter pressure as a leader, but *when*. Regrettably, we live in a world where too many people have risen to a position of leadership without ever having been placed under pressure. When the inevitable occurs, and pressure hits with a vengeance, many leaders simply find themselves overwhelmed.

As scientifically defined, pressure is the ratio of force to the area over which said force is distributed or applied. But pressure has an impact that reaches well beyond the scientific realm. Pressure can also represent the effect of a force applied against a person's values, positions, philosophies, and even their will to survive. Too much pressure applied to an unwilling, unprepared, ill-equipped, or incapable leader results in flawed thinking, bad decisions, and wrong actions.

In and of itself, pressure is neither good nor bad. Dealing with pressure is little more than a state of mind. Some see leadership as a privilege and others see it as a burden—I tend to view leadership as a burden of privilege. Nevertheless, nobody is immune to pressure; some just handle it better than others. But here's the thing—how leaders deal with pressure is often the difference between catapulting an organization towards success, and contributing to its demise. The right perspective on pressure can create a very positive new normal.

It's been my experience that good leaders place such high levels of pressure on themselves that external pressures seem almost trivial by comparison. I consistently place pressure on myself to be a better leader and a better person—this focuses my efforts and provides a source of intrinsic motivation far beyond any extrinsic pressure others could ever exert upon me.

Following are six things smart leaders do that transform pressure from a liability to an asset:

1. **Know Thyself:** Leaders must know themselves, their strengths and weaknesses, and where they will and won't compromise. When leaders are comfortable in their own skin, they won't fear dissenting opinion and diversity of thought—they'll encourage it. Knowing who you are frees you to become a better thinker and a better leader.

2. **Lead:** A leader's job is to acquire and develop talent. The larger the organization you lead, the more your performance is dependent upon the talent of your team. The better the talent, and the better you utilize talent, the less pressure you'll feel. The key to capacity, throughput, and scale is not found by doing—but by developing others to do. Leaders who feel the least amount of pressure are those who spend the most time acquiring and developing talent. Conversely, leaders who feel the most pressure are those who feel they must do everything themselves.

3. **Keep It Simple:** Complexity creates pressure. The best leaders look to simplify everything they can. Simplicity rarely equates to a lack of sophistication—it actually demonstrates remarkable elegance. Simplicity drives understanding, which leads to a certainty of execution. One truism you can count on is that performance relives pressure.

4. **Get Alignment:** Great leaders strive for the following: one vision—one team—one agenda. Organizations that have a shared purpose, common values, and aligned interests are simply more productive than organizations that don't. Alignment of values and vision takes the complexity out of decision making, and removes the ambiguity from the process of prioritization. Leaders who have organizational alignment feel less pressure than those who don't.

5. **Focus:** Focused leaders rarely feel external pressure. Unfocused leaders feel as if pressure is coming at them from all directions. Focus affords leaders clarity of thought that a cluttered mind will never realize. It's not possible to lead an organization toward a better future when a leader's mind can't see through the fog. An organization is never under greater pressure, or at greater risk, than when leaders lose their focus.

6. **Create Whitespace:** The best way to maintain focus is to make sure you've baked in some whitespace into *every* day. Any rubber band stretched too tightly will eventually snap—there are no exceptions to this rule. Leaders who don't create time for quality thought and planning end up taking unnecessary short cuts and risks. They let pressure force them into making bad decisions that a little whitespace could have prevented.

Never underestimate the value of talent. Leaders who undervalue or underutilize talent will be replaced by those who don't.

Hacking the Turnover Gap

No discussion on the topic of talent would be complete without discussing the problems associated with employee turnover. Have you ever noticed leaders spend a lot of time talking about talent, only to make the same mistakes over and over again? It's undeniable that few things in business are as costly and disruptive as unexpected talent departures. With all the emphasis on leadership development, I always find it interesting that so many companies seem to struggle with being able to retain their top talent.

Ask CEOs if they have a process for retaining and developing talent, and they'll quickly answer in the affirmative. They immediately launch into a series of sound bites about the quality of their talent initiatives, the number of high-potentials in the nine box, blah, blah, blah. As with most things in the corporate world, there is too much process built upon theory and not nearly enough practice built on experience.

When examining the talent at any organization look at the culture, not the rhetoric—look at the results, not the commentary about potential. Despite some of the delusional perspective in the corner office, when we interview their employees, here's what they tell us:

- More than 30 percent believe they'll be working someplace else inside of 12 months.
- More than 40 percent don't respect the person they report to.
- More than 50 percent say they have different values from their employer.
- More than 60 percent don't feel their career goals are aligned with the plans their employers have for them.
- More than 70 percent don't feel appreciated or valued by their employer.

So, for all those employers who *have everything under control*, you better start reevaluating. There is an old saying that goes: "Employees don't quit working for companies, they quit working for their bosses." Regardless of tenure, position, title, and so on, employees who voluntarily leave, generally do so out of some type of perceived disconnect with leadership.

Here's the thing—employees who are challenged, engaged, valued, and rewarded (emotionally, intellectually, and financially) rarely leave, and, more importantly, they perform at very high levels. However, if you miss any of these critical areas, it's only a matter of time until they head for the elevator. Following are 10 reasons your talent will leave you—smart leaders don't make these mistakes:

1. **You Failed to Unleash Their Passions:** Smart companies align employee passions with corporate pursuits. Human nature makes it very difficult to walk away from areas of passion. Fail to understand this, and you'll unknowingly be encouraging employees to seek their passions elsewhere.

2. **You Failed to Challenge Their Intellect:** Smart people don't like to live in a dimly lit world of boredom. If you don't challenge people's minds, they'll leave you for someone/someplace that will.

3. **You Failed to Engage Their Creativity:** Great talent is wired to improve, enhance, and add value. They are built to change and innovate. They *need* to contribute by putting their fingerprints on design. Smart leaders don't place people in boxes—they free them from boxes. What's the use in having racehorses if you don't let them run?

4. **You Failed to Develop Their Skills:** Leadership isn't a destination—it's a continuum. No matter how smart or talented a person is, there's always room for growth, development, and continued maturation. If you place restrictions on people's ability to grow, they'll leave you for someone who won't.

5. **You Failed to Give Them a Voice:** Talented people have good thoughts, ideas, insights, and observations. If you don't listen to them, I can guarantee you someone else will.

6. **You Failed to Care:** Sure, people come to work for a paycheck, but that's not the only reason. In fact, many studies show it's not even the most important reason. If you fail to care about people at a human level, at an emotional level, they'll eventually leave you, regardless of how much you pay them.

7. **You Failed to Lead:** Businesses don't fail, products don't fail, projects don't fail, and teams don't fail—leaders fail. The best testament to the value of leadership is what happens in its absence—very little. If you fail to lead, your talent will seek leadership elsewhere.

8. **You Failed to Recognize Their Contributions:** The best leaders don't take credit—they give it. Failing to recognize the contributions of others is not only arrogant and disingenuous, but it's as also just as good as asking them to leave.

9. **You Failed to Increase Their Responsibility:** You cannot confine talent—try to do so and you'll either devolve into mediocrity

or force your talent to seek more fertile ground. People will gladly accept a huge workload as long as an increase in responsibility comes along with the performance and execution of said workload.

10. **You Failed to Keep Your Commitments:** Promises made are worthless, but promises kept are invaluable. If you break trust with those you lead, you will pay a very steep price. While I shared the following thought with you earlier, it's worth noting here again: Leaders not accountable *to* their people will eventually be held accountable *by* their people.

If leaders spent less time trying to retain people, and more time trying to understand them, care for them, invest in them, and lead them well, the retention thing would take care of itself.

Chapter 7

Hacking the Knowledge Gap

The most profoundly overlooked aspect of learning is
recognizing the necessity of unlearning.

K nowledge matters; but when it comes to leadership, knowledge isn't about being right—it's about achieving the right
outcomes. Here's the thing: No one has all the answers, so why
even attempt to pretend that you do? The biggest barrier to the acquisition, distribution, and application of knowledge is a leader's ego. While
the best leaders possess several hacks to deal with personal and organizational knowledge gaps, the most important hack is for leaders to get out
of their own way and out of the way of those they lead.

It is an organization's ability to collect and convert data into information, turn information into knowledge, and knowledge into an operating advantage that allows an enterprise to effectively address current
needs as well as to strategically drive innovation and forward planning.

Put more simply, a corporation's employees must be able to acquire knowledge (learning), transfer knowledge (out of the head and into an information system), apply knowledge (from the information system into an actionable event), manage knowledge (execute with focus, timing, and precision), and secure knowledge (keep it from evaporating or even worse from walking out the door to a competitor).

Some would say we've moved from information and knowledge workers to entire knowledge enterprises. While this may be true, all the institutional knowledge in the world won't protect you from leaders who can't separate useful knowledge from useless knowledge, and from leaders who don't know how to leverage knowledge into competitive advantage.

Hacking Static Thinking

I love vigorous debate, generally have an open mind, and actually enjoy having my thoughts and opinions challenged. If everyone always agreed with me conversation wouldn't be very stimulating, and acquiring new knowledge and insight would certainly be more difficult.

That said, I only really have the patience for intellectually honest discourse. I don't care in the slightest about winning arguments, whether someone is right or wrong, or whether logic is sound or flawed, but I do care about motivation and intent. In the text that follows I'm going to ask you to do some soul searching—up for the challenge?

Smart leaders don't tell people what they should think; they surround themselves with great thinkers, and then consistently seek their insights, observations, and opinions. Subjecting yourself to dissenting opinion allows you to refine your good ideas, weed out the bad ideas, and acquire new ideas. Moreover, it's the ability to evolve and to nuance thinking that leads to the change and innovation your organization needs to survive.

Show me people who never change their minds, and I'll show you static thinkers who have sentenced their minds to a prison of mediocrity and wasted potential. If the world is constantly changing, if the marketplace is always evolving, if the minds of others are continuously developing, how can you attempt to be unchanging and still be relevant? The smartest people I know are the most willing to change their minds. They don't want to be right, they want the right outcome—they want to learn, grow, develop, and mature.

A leader's ability to change his or her mind demonstrates humility, confidence and maturity. It makes them approachable, and it makes them human. People are looking for authentic, transparent leaders willing to sacrifice their ego in favor of right thinking. Bottom line—when you fear being wrong more than being proven wrong, you have arrived as a leader.

A few initial questions to ponder as we get started—How do you react when someone disagrees with you? Do you tuck tail and run desiring to avoid conflict at all costs? Do you dig in your heels and prepare to defend your position to the death, all the while not really caring about how many casualties are incurred in the process? Or do you attempt to gain knowledge, understanding, and perspective? Most importantly, do you genuinely engage in pursuit of the truth, or do you just wax eloquent in an attempt to justify your opinion or position?

It seems today's world is awash with people who have lost the ability to disagree with others, yet still respect them. If people challenge your thinking and you immediately view them as an adversary, there might be a problem with your perspective. Are your leadership skills developed enough to have the tough conversations, or just the conversations you want to have?

Here's my premise—few things benefit leaders in the ways that dissenting opinions do. The best leaders constantly seek out and engage those who challenge their thinking. They are curious, inquisitive, and have an insatiable appetite for learning. Most importantly, they truly care about what others think and why they hold the convictions they do.

Whether you see opposing views and positions as conflict or opportunity says a lot about you as a person, and especially gives insightful commentary on who you are as a leader. Being able to discern and debate subjective positions with objectivity is an art form that must be present for effective leadership. If you cannot lead someone with whom you disagree, then you are not a leader—you're a dictator. If you cannot surround yourself with those who challenge your thinking, then you are not a leader—you're an egomaniac.

Understanding and respecting others' perceptions is such a critical part of being an effective leader that absent this ability, I truly believe you cannot be effective in a leadership role. Great leaders take the time to understand the various constituencies and spheres of influence they come in contact with. "My way or the highway" thinking, and/or positional dictatorships rarely create the culture and performance demonstrated by winning organizations.

While I long ago reached the conclusion that perception does in fact matter, it may not be for the reasons that you may think. I have found that the majority of people tend to be myopic with regard to perception; they understand their own perceptions, but are quite often either ignorant or uncompassionate with regard to the perceptions of others. You see, the most important item to understand is that success as a leader has very little to do with your perception, but rather it has everything to do with the perception of others.

I'm not suggesting that you ignore your perception, subordinate your perception, or change your perception, but I am strongly suggesting that you take the time to both be aware of, and understand the perceptions of others. What I've just espoused has nothing to with compromising your values or being disingenuous. Rather my reasoning simply hypothesizes that if you're not in touch with the perceptions of meaningful constituencies, your success will be impeded by your tunnel vision.

When it comes to authentic, transparent discourse, motivations matter. Those who place the care and regard of others above advancing their personal, positional, professional, or political agendas will garner trust, respect, and influence. You see it is precisely by not attempting to steamroll, manipulate, or outsmart others, that you'll be able to effectively convey your message even to an audience that might not otherwise be willing or receptive. Moreover, by having open and honest interactions you might actually learn something.

I can guarantee you that you're not always right, that your thinking can be nuanced, that your knowledge can be deepened, that you can reframe and evolve your positions, and that your vision can be expanded. However, these things don't generally happen if you give monologues rather than participate in dialogues.

If you don't engage those who hold dissenting opinions and viewpoints in candid and open discussions, you will struggle in developing to your true intellectual potential. Whether you agree or disagree is not the point. The point is that understanding the perceptions of others affords you a source of intelligence, a learning opportunity, and the ability to keep lines of communication open.

Hacking the Decision Gap

The great benefit of knowledge and experience is the hope that they will lead to wisdom. The best leaders use their knowledge to not only make better decisions for themselves, but to help those they lead to make better decisions.

The one thing everyone on the planet has in common is the undeniable fact we've all made our fair share of regrettable decisions. Show me someone who hasn't made a bad decision, and I'll show you someone who is either not being honest, or someone who avoids decisioning at all costs.

Making sound decisions is a skill set that needs to be developed like any other. As a person who works with CEOs on a daily basis, I can tell you with great certainty all leaders are not created equal when it comes to the competency of their decisioning skills. Nothing will test your leadership mettle more than your ability to make decisions.

Why do leaders fail? They make poor choices that lead to bad decisions. And in some cases they compound bad decision upon bad decision. You cannot separate leadership from decisioning, for like it or not, they are inexorably linked. Put simply, the outcome of leaders' choices and decisions can, and usually will, make or break them.

The fact of the matter is most leaders who rapidly progress in their career path do so largely based upon their ability to consistently make sound decisions. What most fail to realize is years of solid decision making is oftentimes unwound by a single bad decision. As much as you may wish it wasn't so, when it comes to being a leader you're really only as good as your last decision.

Here's the thing—even leaders who don't fail make bad decisions from time to time. When I reflect back upon the poor decisions I've made, it's not that I wasn't capable of making the correct decision, but for whatever reason I failed to use sound decisioning methodology. Gut instincts can only take you so far in life, and anyone who operates outside of a sound-decisioning framework will eventually fall prey to an act of oversight, misinformation, misunderstanding, manipulation, impulsivity, or some other negative influencing factor.

The first key in understanding how to make great decisions is learning how to synthesize the overwhelming amount of incoming information leaders must deal with on a daily basis, while making the best decisions possible in a timely fashion. The key to dealing with the voluminous amounts of information is as simple as becoming better at the filtering of various inputs.

Understanding that a hierarchy of knowledge exists is critically important when attempting to make prudent decisions. News Flash— not all inputs should weigh equally in one's decisioning process. By developing a qualitative and quantitative filtering mechanism for decision making, you can make better decisions in a shorter period of time. The hierarchy of knowledge is as follows:

- **Gut Instincts:** This is an experiential and/or emotional filter that may oftentimes have no current underpinning of hard analytical support. That said, in absence of other decisioning filters it can sometimes be all a person has to go on when making a decision. Even when more refined analytics are available, your instincts can often provide a very valuable gut check against the reasonability or bias of other inputs. The big takeaway here is that intuitive decisioning can be refined and improved. My advice is to actually work at becoming very discerning.
- **Data:** Raw data is comprised of disparate facts, statistics, or random inputs that in and of themselves hold little value. Making conclusions based on data in its raw form will lead to flawed decisions based on incomplete data sets.
- **Information:** Information is simply an evolved or more complete data set. Information is therefore derived from a collection of processed data where context and meaning have been added to disparate facts, which allow for a more thorough analysis.
- **Knowledge:** Knowledge is information that has been refined by analysis such that it has been assimilated, tested and/or validated.

Most importantly, knowledge is actionable with a high degree of accuracy because proof of concept exists.

Even though people often treat theory and opinion as fact, they are not one and the same. I have witnessed many a savvy executive blur the lines between fact and fiction resulting in an ill-advised decision when decisions are made under extreme pressure and outside of a sound-decisioning framework. Decisions made at the gut instinct or data level can be made quickly, but offer a higher level of risk. Decisioning at the information level affords a higher degree of risk management, but is still not as safe as those decisions based upon actionable knowledge.

Another aspect that needs to be factored into the decisioning process is the *source* of the input. I believe it was Cyrus the Great who said "diversity in counsel, unity in command," meaning that good leaders seek the counsel of others, but maintain control over the final decision. While most successful leaders subscribe to this theory, the real question is not whether you should seek counsel, but in fact where and how much counsel you should seek.

You see, more input, or the wrong input, doesn't necessarily add value to a decisioning process. Volume for the sake of volume will only tend to confuse matters, and seeking input from sources that can't offer significant contributions is likely a waste of time. Two other issues should be considered in your decisioning process as they relate to the source of input:

1. **Credibility:** What is the track record of your source? Is the source reliable and credible? Are they delivering data, information, or knowledge? Will the source tell you what you want to hear, what they want you to hear, or will they provide the unedited version of cold, hard truth?

2. **Bias:** Are there any hidden and/or competing agendas that are coloring the input being received? Is the input being provided for the benefit of the source or the benefit of the enterprise?

The complexity of the current business landscape, combined with ever increasing expectations of performance, and the speed at which decisions must be made, are a potential recipe for disaster for today's executive unless a defined methodology for decisioning is put into place. If you incorporate the following six metrics into your decisioning framework, you will minimize the chances of making a bad decision:

1. **Perform a Situation Analysis:** What is motivating the need for a decision? What would happen if no decision is made? Who will the decision impact (both directly and indirectly)? What data, analytics, research, or supporting information do you have to validate the inclinations driving your decision?

2. **Subject Your Decision to Public Scrutiny:** There are no private decisions. Sooner or later, the details surrounding any decision will likely come out. If your decision were printed on the front page of the newspaper, how would you feel? What would your family think of your decision? How would your shareholders and employees feel about your decision? Have you sought counsel and/or feedback before making your decision?

3. **Conduct a Cost/Benefit Analysis:** Do the potential benefits derived from the decision justify the expected costs? What if the costs exceed projections and the benefits fall short of projections?

4. **Assess the Risk/Reward Ratio:** What are all the possible rewards, and when contrasted with all the potential risks, are the odds in your favor, or are they stacked against you?

5. **Assess Whether It Is the Right Thing to Do:** Standing behind decisions that everyone supports doesn't particularly require a lot of chutzpah. On the other hand, standing behind what one believes is the right decision in the face of tremendous controversy is the stuff great leaders are made of. My wife has always told me that "you can't go wrong by going right," and as usual, I find her advice to be spot on. There are many areas where compromise yields significant benefits, but your value system, your character, or your integrity should never be compromised.

6. **Make the Decision:** Perhaps most importantly, you must have a bias toward action and be willing to make the decision. Moreover, you must learn to make the best decision possible, even if you possess an incomplete data set. Don't fall prey to analysis paralysis, but rather make the best decision possible with the information at hand using some of the methods mentioned above. Opportunities are not static, and the law of diminishing returns applies to most

opportunities in that the longer you wait to seize the opportunity, the smaller the return typically is. In fact, more likely is the case that the opportunity will completely evaporate if you wait too long to seize it.

Bonus—Always Have a Back-Up Plan: The real test of leaders is what happens in the moments following the realization they've made the wrong decision. Great leaders understand all plans are made up of both constants and variables, and that sometimes the variables work against you. Smart leaders always have a contingency plan, knowing circumstances can sometimes fall beyond the boundaries of reason or control—no "Plan B" equals a flawed plan.

Smart leaders learn to make good decisions, and then they teach others to do the same.

Hacking the Competency Gap

The pendulum that swings back and forth between generalist and specialist has in recent history never swung to a more extreme position. The fact is we live in a time of hyperspecialization. There are specialists for everything—even areas that don't require them. This over emphasis has led us to a place where competency is overvalued.

When organizations hire, develop, and promote leaders using a competency-based model, they're unwittingly incubating failure. Nothing fractures corporate culture faster, and eviscerates talent development efforts more rapidly, than rewarding the wrong people for the wrong reasons. Don't reward technical competency in a vacuum— reward aggregate contribution.

Any organization that over weights the importance of technical competency fails to recognize the considerable and often-untapped value contained in the whole of the person. It's the cumulative power of a person's soft skills, the sum of the parts if you will, that creates real value. It's not what a person knows so much as it is how they're able to use said knowledge to inspire and create brilliance in others that really matters.

We live in a time that has moved well beyond competency-driven models, yet organizations still primarily use competency-based interviews, competency-based development, competency-based performance reviews, and competency-based rewards as their framework for doing business. It remains the *best* practices mentality that rules the day, when we're long overdue for a shift to *next* practices. It's simply not possible to change current behaviors by refusing to embrace new paradigms.

Sure corporations know the right buzzwords—they pay lip service to things like character, trust, passion, purpose, EQ, collaboration, creativity, and so on, but they really don't value them in the same way they value competency. One of the problems is competency is predictable and easy to measure, and corporations like predictable and easy. However, just because something is easy to measure doesn't mean it's the right thing to measure, and certainly not when measured in a vacuum.

Competency should represent nothing more than table stakes—it should be assumed. Having the requisite level of competency to do your job is not to be rewarded—it's to be expected. The train is really off the tracks when being technically and/or functionally qualified to do a job makes you a high potential.

The value organizations should be cultivating and curating in people is their ability to align purpose, vision, values, character, and commitment with demonstrated competency. Competency isn't the entirety of a person's worth, and it certainly shouldn't be the gold standard of their measurement. It's a small part of the equation, but in many cases corporations treat it as if it's the only thing that matters.

Here's the thing—you can possess the greatest technical wizardry under the stars, but that doesn't make you a leader. If you don't care, aren't collaborative, can't communicate, fail to take input and feedback, and allow your hubris to overshadow your humility, you might be intelligent, but in my book (no pun intended) you're not very bright. The really sad part of this story is how often this type of person is rewarded in a competency-based system.

We must recognize competency-based leadership models simply don't work. They are deeply rooted in the foundations of command and control structures, and they've outgrown the value they afforded organizations as nations moved beyond the industrial era. Competency-based models simply create alignment gaps at every level—organizational gaps, talent gaps, leadership gaps, cultural gaps, diversity gaps, positional gaps, value gaps, operational gaps, execution gaps, and the list could go on. A leader's job is to close gaps—not create them.

If you want to create a true culture of leadership, it's necessary to actually lead. Smart thinking and acting must start to take precedence over soaring rhetoric. It takes more than paying lip service to a few soft skills on a performance scorecard to get the job done. It will take a cultural shift in actually understanding, recognizing, and rewarding what we say we value.

The bottom line is this—the people who spend the most time complaining about the lack of talent are the ones who don't recognize talent to begin with—don't be that person.

Hacking the Learning Gap

The minute you stop learning you stop leading. The question is how do you ensure people and organizations continue learning in an effective manner? Over the years, I've observed just about every type of leadership development program on the planet. And the sad thing is, most of them don't even come close to accomplishing what they were designed to do—build better leaders.

According to the American Society of Training and Development, U.S. businesses spend more than $170 billion on leadership-based curricula, with the majority of those dollars being spent on "Leadership Training." Here's the thing—when it comes to leadership, the training industry has been broken for years. You don't train leaders; you develop them—a subtle yet important distinction lost on many. Leadership training is alive and well, but it should have died long, long ago.

This may be heresy to some—but training is indeed the number-one reason leadership development fails. While training is often accepted as productive, it rarely is. The terms *training* and *development* have somehow become synonymous when they are clearly not. This is more than an argument based on semantics—it's painfully real.

An Overview of the Problem: My problem with training is that it *presumes* the need for indoctrination on systems, processes, and techniques. Moreover, training *assumes* that said systems, processes, and techniques are the right way to do things. When a trainer refers to something as "best practices," you can with great certitude rest assured that's not the case. Training focuses on best practices, while development focuses on next practices. Training is often a rote, one-directional, one-dimensional, one-size-fits-all, authoritarian process that imposes static, outdated information on people. The majority of training takes place within a monologue (lecture/presentation) rather than a dialog. Perhaps worst of all, training usually occurs within a vacuum driven by past experience, not by future needs.

The Solution: The solution to the leadership training problem is to scrap it in favor of development. Don't train leaders, coach them, mentor them, disciple them, and develop them, but please don't attempt to train them. Where training attempts to standardize by blending to a norm and acclimating to the status quo, development strives to call out the unique, and differentiate by shattering the status quo. Training is something leaders dread and will try and avoid, whereas they will embrace and look forward to development. Development is nuanced, contextual, collaborative, fluid, and above all else, actionable.

The following 20 items point out some of the main differences between training and development:

1. Training blends to a norm—Development occurs beyond the norm.
2. Training focuses on technique/content/curriculum—Development focuses on people.
3. Training tests patience—Development tests courage.
4. Training focuses on the present—Development focuses on the future.
5. Training adheres to standards—Development focuses on maximizing potential.
6. Training is transactional—Development is transformational.
7. Training focuses on maintenance—Development focuses on growth.
8. Training focuses on the role—Development focuses on the person.
9. Training indoctrinates—Development educates.
10. Training maintains the status quo—Development catalyzes innovation.
11. Training stifles culture—Development enriches culture.
12. Training encourages compliance—Development emphasizes performance.
13. Training focuses on efficiency—Development focuses on effectiveness.
14. Training focuses on problems—Development focuses on solutions.
15. Training focuses on reporting lines—Development expands influence.

16. Training places people in a box—Development frees them from the box.
17. Training is mechanical—Development is intellectual.
18. Training focuses on the knowns—Development explores the unknowns.
19. Training places people in a comfort zone—Development moves people beyond their comfort zones.
20. Training is finite—Development is infinite.

If what you desire is robotic, static thinkers—train them. If you're seeking innovative, critical thinkers—develop them. I have always said it is impossible to have an enterprise that is growing and evolving if leadership is not.

Hacking the Reading Gap

It might sound strange to talk about a reading gap, but this is one area that many leaders could improve upon. Did you know that the average American reads only one book a year? Worse than this is the fact that 60 percent of average Americans only get through the first chapter. Contrast this with the fact that CEOs of Fortune 500 companies read an average of four to five books a month. Even more impressive is that some of the most successful leaders throughout history were known to read one book every single day. Bottom line: If you're a leader and not an avid reader, *you're wrong*.

If the statistics in the opening paragraph didn't convince you of the power of reading, here are a few more telling observations for your consideration—according to our surveys at N2growth, a very large common denominator shared by executives who feel that they are not achieving the level of success they feel capable of, is that many of them are "too busy to keep up with their reading." Hmmm. . . . Furthermore, studies show that active readers are likely to have annual incomes more than five times greater than those who spend little or no time reading. Do I have your attention yet?

Up until a few years ago, Rick Warren read a book every single day. Abraham Lincoln, who only had one year of formal education, credited his appetite for reading with his success. Teddy Roosevelt was rumored to actually read two books a day. Thomas Jefferson had one of the most exhaustive personal libraries of his time prior to donating it to the Library of Congress (which many joked Roosevelt had read). If not clear yet, the theme here is that in order to be a great leader, you absolutely must be a great reader.

As an advisor to CEOs, there is little doubt that I'm passionate about personal and professional development, and there is one simple reason why—it works. Great leaders are like a sponge when it comes to the acquisition of knowledge, and the development of new skill sets. To the person, the best leaders I know are prolific readers. The most successful people I know consume written content at a pace that far exceeds that of the average person. If you want to improve your station in life, as well as the lives around you—read more.

While there are certainly numerous ways to learn (observation, experience, classroom instruction, relational interactions, and so on), I am a huge fan of the benefits of professional development gained from good old-fashioned reading. Someone once said, "You are what you read," and while I think there is far more to the equation of our individual makeup than our choice of reading material, the statistics mentioned above prove there is also an element of truth contained in the aforementioned quote.

If I told you how much time I spend reading and researching, you probably wouldn't believe me, but suffice it to say, I am a voracious reader. I will often read a book in one sitting, have more than a dozen books presently underway on my Kindle, subscribe to online clipping services, use RSS feeds to scour news groups and forums. I devour social content on blogs, podcasts, Twitter, Facebook, various iPhone apps, and so on, and this is in addition to reading a variety of industry publications and periodicals.

With what I've noted thus far I'm always amazed at the number of executives who don't keep up with their professional reading. To be blunt, I have little patience for those leaders who are "too busy" or "too smart" or "too important" to learn. Put simply, if you're not learning, you have no business leading. How can you possibly be expected to grow an organization if you're not growing yourself? How can you accept the responsibility to develop a team if you're not developing yourself?

The greatest leaders throughout history have been nothing short of relentless in their pursuit of knowledge. If you are anything less, then you are not only cheating yourself, but you're also cheating your organization. I believe Michelangelo said it best when he uttered the words "Ancora Imparo," which when translated from the Italian means "I am still learning." By the way, his first public use of this phrase was noted to have been on his 87th birthday. I don't know about you, but I'm still learning. Moreover, the day I stop reading, the day I stop learning— that's the day I stop leading and likely the day I stop breathing.

Let me take this opportunity to disabuse any misconceptions that may exist when I mention acquiring knowledge. I'm not promoting intellectual elitism, rather I'm espousing the benefits that are derived by those who have a true and sincere passion for learning . . . there is a difference. Intellectual elitists are by and large braggarts that acquire knowledge (or feign possession thereof) for public acclaim and their own self-promotion. Learning serves little purpose for leaders if it is not actionable. If you acquire knowledge, yet choose not to use it for the benefit of others, then you're not a leader, you're self-indulgent.

In concurrence with Michelangelo's quote above, I have never been a believer in the adage "you can't teach an old dog new tricks." In fact, quite to the contrary; I believe anyone (yes, I mean anyone) can change/learn/grow/develop given one prerequisite: the desire to do so. When it comes to topic of learning, it has been my experience that there are generally three types of people: those who constantly seek to acquire knowledge, those who think they already know it all, and those who just don't care. What distinguishes members of one group from another rarely has anything to do with intellect, wealth, social pedigree, career standing, or other like pursuits. It has everything to do with desire.

Reading should not be something that is done when you're bored, or have nothing better to do; rather it needs to be incorporated into your daily regimen. I have personally worked with literally hundreds of C-suite executives and without question the most successful professionals are those that constantly seek out learning opportunities and who are voracious readers.

They realize the importance of learning and make reading a priority. Think of the business leaders that have had the biggest positive impact in your life, and I'm sure you'll find that these individuals were in constant search of new and better information. They use the information acquired through reading in order to inspire, motivate, and lead those around them.

Whether young or old, experienced or inexperienced, the best way to approach personal and professional development is to always stay in the learning zone. When you think you have all the answers is when you are headed straight for the proverbial brick wall. That said, most things in life happen as a result of choices we make. It is clearly within your grasp to make the choice to gain an understanding of what it is that you don't know, and determine how you want to deal with that situation. My recommendation is simple, if you want to increase your income, your impact, or your influence, then I would suggest you increase your reading.

Hacking the Communication Gap

When it comes to knowledge, it really doesn't matter how much you know if you cannot communicate it to others. It is simply impossible to become a great leader without being a great communicator. I hope you noticed the previous sentence didn't refer to being a great talker—big difference.

The key to becoming a skillful communicator is rarely found in what has been taught in the world of academia. From our earliest days in the classroom, we are trained to focus on enunciation, vocabulary, presence, delivery, grammar, syntax, and the like. In other words, we are taught to focus on ourselves. While I don't mean to belittle these things, as they're important to learn, it's the more subtle elements of communication rarely taught in the classroom (the elements that focus on others) that leaders desperately need to learn.

It is the ability to develop a keen external awareness that separates the truly great communicators from those who muddle through their interactions with others. Examine the world's greatest leaders, and you'll find them all to be exceptional communicators. They may talk about their ideas, but they do so in a way that also speaks to your emotions and your aspirations. They realize that if their message doesn't take deep root with the audience then it likely won't be understood, much less championed.

I don't believe it comes as any great surprise that most leaders spend the overwhelming majority of their time each day in some type of an interpersonal situation. I also don't believe it comes as a great shock that a large number of organizational problems occur as a result of poor communications. It is precisely this paradox that underscores the need for leaders to focus on becoming great communicators.

Effective communication is an essential component of professional success, whether it is at the interpersonal, intergroup, intragroup, organizational, or external level. While developing an understanding of great communication skills is easier than one might think, being able to appropriately draw upon said skills when the chips are down is not always as easy as one might hope for.

Skills acquired and/or knowledge gained are only valuable to the extent they can be practically applied when called for. The number one thing great communicators have in common is they possess a heightened sense of situational and contextual awareness. The best communicators are great listeners, and they are astute in their observations.

Great communicators are skilled at reading a person/group by sensing the moods, dynamics, attitudes, values, and concerns of those being communicated with. Not only do they read their environment well, but they possess the uncanny ability to adapt their messaging to this environment without missing a beat. The message is not about the messenger; it has nothing to do with messenger; it is however 100 percent about meeting the needs and the expectations of those you're communicating with.

So, how do you know when your skills have matured to the point that you've become an excellent communicator? The answer is that you'll have reached the point where your interactions with others consistently take advantage of the following 10 principles:

1. **Speak Not with a Forked Tongue:** In most cases, people just won't open up to those they don't trust. When people have a sense a leader is worthy of their trust, they will invest time and take risks in ways they never would if their leader had a reputation built upon poor character or lack of integrity. While you can attempt to

demand trust, it rarely works. Trust is best created when it's earned through right acting, thinking, and decisioning. Keep in mind people will forgive many things where trust exists, but will rarely forgive anything where trust is absent.

2. **Get Personal:** Stop issuing corporate communications and begin having organizational conversations—think dialogue not monologue. Here's the thing—the more personal and engaging the conversation is, the more effective it will be. There is great truth in the following axiom: "People don't care how much you know until they know how much you care." Classic business theory tells leaders to stay at arm's length. I say stay at arm's length if you want to remain in the dark, receiving only highly sanitized versions of the truth. If you don't develop meaningful relationships with people, you'll never know what's really on their mind until it's too late to do anything about it.

3. **Get Specific:** Specificity is better than ambiguity 11 times out of 10: Learn to communicate with clarity. Simple and concise is always better than complicated and confusing. Time has never been a more precious commodity than it is today. It is critical that leaders learn how to cut to the chase and hit the high points—it's also important to expect the same from others. Without understanding the value of brevity and clarity, it is unlikely you'll ever be afforded the opportunity to get to the granular level as people will tune you out long before you ever get there. Your goal is to weed out the superfluous and to make your words count.

4. **Focus on the Leave-Behinds, Not the Takeaways:** The best communicators are not only skilled at learning and gathering information while communicating, they are also adept at transferring ideas, aligning expectations, inspiring action, and spreading their vision. The key is to approach each interaction with a servant's heart. When you truly focus on contributing more than receiving, you will have accomplished the goal. Even though this may seem counterintuitive, by intensely focusing on the other party's wants, needs, and desires, you'll learn far more than you ever would by focusing on your agenda.

5. **Have an Open Mind:** I've often said that the rigidity of a closed mind is the single greatest limiting factor of new opportunities.

Leaders take their game to a whole new level the minute they willingly seek out those who hold dissenting opinions and opposing positions with the goal not of convincing them to change their minds, but with the goal of understanding what's on their mind. I'm always amazed at how many people are truly fearful of opposing views, when what they should be is genuinely curious and interested. Open dialogues with those who confront you, challenge you, stretch you, and develop you. Remember that it's not the opinion that matters, but rather the willingness to discuss it with an open mind and learn.

6. **Shut Up and Listen:** Great leaders know when to dial it up, dial it down, and dial it off (mostly down and off). Simply broadcasting your message ad nauseam will not have the same result as engaging in meaningful conversation, but this assumes that you understand that the greatest form of discourse takes place within a conversation, and not a lecture or a monologue. When you reach that point in your life where the light bulb goes off, and you begin to understand that knowledge is not gained by flapping your lips, but by removing your ear wax, you have taken the first step to becoming a skilled communicator.

7. **Replace Ego with Empathy:** I have long advised leaders not to let their ego write checks that their talent can't cash. When candor is communicated with empathy and caring and not the prideful arrogance of an over inflated ego, good things begin to happen. Empathetic communicators display a level of authenticity and transparency that is not present with those who choose to communicate behind the carefully crafted facade propped-up by a very fragile ego. Understanding this communication principle is what helps turn anger into respect and doubt into trust.

8. **Read between the Lines:** Take a moment and reflect back on great leaders that come to mind. You'll find they are very adept at reading between the lines. They have the uncanny ability to understand what is not said, witnessed, or heard. Being a leader should not be viewed as a license to increase the volume of rhetoric. Instead, astute leaders know that there is far more to be gained by surrendering the floor than by filibustering. In this age of instant communication, people seem to be in such a rush to communicate what's

on their minds that they fail to realize everything to be gained from the minds of others. Keep your eyes and ears open and your mouth shut, and you'll be amazed at how your level or organizational awareness is raised.

9. **When You Speak, Know What You're Talking About:** Develop a technical command over your subject matter. If you don't possess subject matter expertise, few people will give you the time of day. Most successful people have little interest in listening to those individuals who cannot add value to a situation or topic, but force themselves into a conversation just to hear themselves speak. "The fake it until you make it" days have long since passed, and for most people I know fast and slick equals not credible. You've all heard the saying, "It's not what you say, but how you say it that matters"; and while there is surely an element of truth in that statement, I'm here to tell you that it matters very much what you say. Good communicators address both the *what* and *how* aspects of messaging so they don't fall prey to becoming the smooth talker who leaves people with the impression of form over substance.

10. **Speak to Groups as Individuals:** Leaders don't always have the luxury of speaking to individuals in an intimate setting. Great communicators can tailor a message such that they can speak to 10 people in a conference room or 10,000 people in an auditorium and have them feel as if they were speaking directly to each one of them as an individual. Knowing how to work a room and establish credibility, trust, and rapport are keys to successful interactions.

Bonus—Be Prepared to Change the Message if Needed: Another component of communications strategy that is rarely discussed is how to prevent a message from going bad, and what to do when it does. It's called being prepared and developing a contingency plan. Again, you must keep in mind that for successful interactions to occur, your objective must be in alignment with those you are communicating with. If your expertise, empathy, clarity, and so forth don't have the desired effect, which by the way is very rare, you need to be able to make an impact by changing things up on the fly. Use great questions, humor, stories, analogies, relevant data, and where needed, bold statements to help connect and engender the confidence and trust that it takes for people to want to engage. While it is sometimes necessary to Shock and Awe, this tactic should be reserved as a last resort.

Don't assume people are ready to have a particular conversation with you just because you're ready to have the conversation with them. Spending time paving the way for a productive conversation is far better than coming off as the proverbial bull in a china shop. Furthermore, you cannot assume anyone knows where you're coming from if you don't tell them. I never ceased to be amazed at how many people assume everyone knows what they want to occur without ever finding it necessary to communicate their objective.

If you fail to justify your message with knowledge, business logic, reason, empathy, and so forth, you will find that said message will likely fall on deaf ears needing reinforcement or clarification afterward.

Hacking the Sensitivity Gap

You'll rarely come across successful leaders who have a tin ear. The best leaders are tuned in to the emotional needs of those they serve. They engage, they listen, they empathize, and they acknowledge. They treat you as a colleague not a subordinate. They seek to understand, not direct. They are not tone deaf—they are relevant because they show they care.

Are you guilty of having a failure to communicate? Here's the thing—who cares if you possess excellent communication skills if you don't use them properly? It simply does no good to listen if you don't hear, or hear if you don't understand. If your engagement isn't advancing your vision, developing your team, or otherwise adding value to your stakeholders, then I would suggest your well-honed skills are not as refined as you may think.

When it comes to communications, it's not just a matter of *if* you send a message that determines whether it's received, but rather *how*, *when*, and *why* you send it that matters. I don't know about you, but I've come across many leaders who just can't seem to put the communications puzzle together—for whatever reason they don't get it. They choose the wrong medium for their message, they appoint the wrong proxy to deliver a message they should have communicated in person, they communicate too infrequently, or my personal pet peeve, they bombard you by communicating far too often with disjointed messages that serve to confuse rather than to clarify—they are tone deaf.

As I've pointed out in other areas of this book, it is simply not possible to be a great leader without being a great communicator. This partially accounts for why we don't encounter great leadership more often. The bottom line is that few things are as important when it comes to leadership as clear, crisp, on-point, and on-time communications. The big miss for most leaders is that they fail to understand that the purpose of communication is not to message, but to engage. It's not about being efficient; it's about making others more effective. It's about focusing on understanding the needs of others.

Put simply, leaders need to figure out the communications rhythms, patterns, and preferences of those they engage with. Leaders must learn to meet their constituents where they are in the manner most likely to add value to their world. The outcome of this should be obvious—improve the world of your stakeholders and your world gets better as well. Focus on the following five points and you'll find that communications, morale, and performance will all improve:

1. **Engage:** Good communications are bidirectional. Don't speak at or to someone—speak with them. Don't monologue—dialogue. While one-way communications might make you feel better initially, they only serve to frustrate those on the receiving end of your messaging. Keep in mind that when the negative impact of your poor communications are felt down the road, the damage will far outweigh the initial ego boost you received from giving your monologue.

2. **Relevance:** I'm always amazed at those who believe just because something matters to them, it must matter to others. Remember that just because you have something to say doesn't necessarily mean other people want to hear it. Furthermore, just increasing the volume or frequency of the message doesn't make it any more relevant. When a message isn't sticking, smart leaders don't raise the volume of the rhetoric—they improve the quality of the message.

3. **Pacing:** It's important to understand that not everyone communicates at the same pace—frequency matters. Again, this isn't easy, but it's well worth the time to figure out. Some people simply require, and are deserving of, more frequent interactions. Likewise, others thrive

on less frequent engagement. Some do well receiving information in group settings, while others require one-on-one time. Moreover, everyone has technology preferences that need to be figured into the equation as well. The important take-away here is that it's *your job* to figure all of this out.

4. **Timing:** Like pacing, it's also important for leaders to understand that timing matters. Just because you have something to say doesn't mean someone is ready or willing to listen. One of the most important things a leader can do is to demonstrate respect for the time of others. Other than in the case of an emergency, interruption is never a good foundation for delivering a message. Whether you're communicating to an audience of one or many, once the audience realizes that you understand their needs and respect their time your message will be much more openly received.

5. **Medium:** I don't really care about my communications preferences, I care about how well my communication is received. I use virtually every communications medium available to me to make sure I meet the needs of my stakeholders. I text, IM, e-mail, phone, tweet, Facebook, blog, use video, and yes, my preference is to go old-school and get face-to-face when possible. I do these things not based upon what works for me, but what works for others. As a result of this, I have learned to make these things work for me. Let me be as clear as I can—a leader who fails to meet the needs of the stakeholders will soon be replaced by a leader who does.

Bottom line—The leadership lesson here is whenever you have a message to communicate (either directly, or indirectly through a third party) make sure said message is true and correct, well-reasoned, and substantiated by solid business logic that is specific, consistent, clear, and accurate. Spending a little extra time on the front-end of the messaging curve will likely save you from considerable aggravation and brain damage on the back-end.

Most importantly of all, keep in mind that communication is not about you, your opinions, your positions, or your circumstances. It's about helping others by meeting their needs, understanding their concerns, and adding value to their world. Do these things and you'll drastically reduce the number of communications problems you'll experience moving forward.

Hacking the Story

I've mentioned storytelling a few times in previous sections, but it's so important in a leader's ability to transfer knowledge that I felt compelled to do a deeper dive. Show me a great leader, and I'll show you a talented storyteller. Leadership and storytelling go hand in hand. In fact, leaders who lack the ability to leverage the power and influence of storytelling are missing the very essence of what accounts for compelling leadership to begin with—*the story*.

If you've ever been captivated by a skilled orator whose articulation and eloquence have influenced your thinking, you understand the power of the art of story. I refer to story as an art form because it is. Storytelling requires talent and practice, but as with any worthy discipline, the investment yields great benefit. A story is the root-level driver behind successfully communicating any message. A subtle side benefit of well-crafted stories can be found in their versatility— they can be delivered in person or by proxy, and in visual, textual, or verbal form.

Before the existence of the written word, learning largely took place by passing down stories through the generations. The passing of history has diluted many things, but not the value of story. Today's technology-driven world has only made it easier to amplify a story— the potential for a story to go viral has never been greater. Here's the thing—you'll never know how good your story is if you choose not to share it. Storytelling is the hook that drives engagement, evokes passion, and provides the energy that fuels innovation. Storytelling is an attraction magnet—it's one thing you definitely want to add to your leadership toolkit.

While an authentic story is much like DNA in that no two stories are exactly the same, it takes more than being unique to be memorable. Stories are the instruments that tug at your emotions, speak to your logic, support your beliefs, and reinforce your positions. Great stories challenge, engage, inform, persuade, entertain, mobilize, convict, and inspire.

Smart leaders understand that stories highlight learning opportunities and create memorable experiences. Are you consciously and consistently using stories to be a more effective leader? Perhaps more importantly, are you scaling storytelling by teaching others how to use stories to their advantage? I'm reminded of a Navy recruiting video, which posed this question: "If someone wrote a story about your life, would anybody read it?" This is a powerful question for any of us to ponder, but especially leaders.

There is no denying everybody loves a good story, and there are numerous reasons why. Think about the novels you've read, movies you've watched, speeches you've listened to, ads that have hooked your interest, or virtually any other message delivered by any other medium, and it's the story that either seals the deal or leaves you feeling cheated. The best part about learning to be a great storyteller is it will afford you the best shot at becoming a story maker. When reflecting on the greatest leaders of our time, you'll quickly see it's their ability to not just tell the story, but their ability to create engagement, inspiration, and influence through their storytelling that sets them apart from the masses.

As a leader, it's your ability to tell a compelling story that sets the tone from the top. Story is the fabric upon which culture is built. It helps you to successfully establish rapport, evangelize a vision, champion a brand, align expectations, build teams, attract talent, assuage concerns, relieve tension, and resolve conflict. A leader's story needs to engender trust while implanting your brand promise in the minds of your various constituencies in a manner that is memorable, authentic, relevant, and actionable. It's the leader's story that allows them to share the color of their experience and the context behind their thinking.

Stories are also quite revealing. Carefully listening to a leader's story will reveal character or a lack thereof. Disingenuous leaders misuse storytelling in an attempt to shield, buffer, distract, lull, or misdirect. They use story to prop up their ego, drive their agenda, and to take aim at their adversaries. The storyline propagated by those playing at leadership is all about them. Their stories are laced with "I" and "my," and their primary focus is to shine the spotlight on themselves.

By contrast, the authentic and appropriate use of story has an outward focus, and is laced with "we" and "our" as the main points of emphasis. Great leaders understand that a story is most powerful when it offers hope and encouragement, when it inspires unification and collaboration, and when it has a humanizing effect. Smart leaders understand storytelling is a highly effective method of creating engagement, opening or extending dialogue, and finding common ground. Perhaps the most valuable use of story is to shine the light on others. Leaders who use the power of story to publicly recognize the contributions of others are simply more successful than those who don't.

So my question is this: Why not incorporate storytelling into your leadership repertoire? While leadership is a complex subject to be sure, it all begins with the story—tell it well and succeed; tell it poorly and fail. This is a simple, yet powerful message I encourage you to take to heart. Nobody will tell your story if you don't first tell it yourself.

Hacking Verbosity

As important as storytelling is, so is listening. While some may be impressed with how well you speak, the right people will be impressed with how well you listen. Great leaders are great listeners, and therefore my message is a simple one—talk less and listen more.

The best leaders are proactive, strategic, and intuitive listeners. They recognize that knowledge and wisdom are not gained by talking, but by listening. Take a moment and reflect back on great leaders who come to mind; you'll find they are very adept at reading between the lines. The best leaders possess the uncanny ability to understand what is not said, witnessed, or heard. *Warning:* This isn't your typical text on listening—it isn't going to coddle you and leave you feeling warm and fuzzy—it is intended for leaders and is rather blunt and to the point.

Want to become a better leader? Stop talking, and start listening. Being a leader should not be viewed as a license to increase the volume of rhetoric. Rather astute leaders know there is far more to be gained by surrendering the floor than by dominating it. In this age of instant communication, people seem to be in such a rush to communicate what's on their mind that they fail to realize the value of everything that can be gleaned from the minds of others. Show me a leader who doesn't recognize the value of listening to others, and I'll show you a train-wreck in the making.

It is simply not possible to be a great leader without being a great communicator. This partially accounts for why we don't encounter great leadership more often. The big miss for most leaders is that they fail to understand that the purpose of communication is not to message, but to engage—*this requires listening*. Don't be fooled into thinking that being heard is more important than hearing. The first rule in communication is to seek understanding before seeking to be understood. Communication is not a one-way street. I've interviewed and worked with some of the most noted leaders of our time, and to the one, they never miss an opportunity to listen. In fact, they aggressively seek out new and better ways to listen.

A key point for all leaders to consider is the immense value contained in the old saying, "It's impossible to stick your foot in your mouth when it's closed." Think about it—when was the last time you viewed a negative sound bite of a CEO who was engaged in active listening?

The next step in the process is learning where to apply your newfound listening skills. Listen to your customers, competitors, your peers, your subordinates, and to those that care about you. Ask people how you can become a better leader, and then *listen*. Take your listening skills online, and don't just push out Tweets and Facebook messages, but ask questions and elicit feedback. Use your vast array of social media platforms, tool sets, and connections to listen. If you follow this advice, not only will you become better informed, but you'll also become more popular with those with whom you interact.

Have you ever walked into an important meeting and wondered who the smartest person in the room was? If you mull this over for a moment you'll find the following statement to be accurate: Almost universally, the smartest person in the room is *not* the one doing all the talking—it's the person asking a few relevant and engaging questions and then doing almost all of the listening. At its essence, leadership is about action. That said, leaders who act before they understand don't tend to achieve the outcomes they desire.

Following are six tips for becoming a better listener:

1. **It's Not about You:** Stop worrying about what you're going to say and focus on what's being said. Don't listen to have your opinions validated or your ego stroked, listen to be challenged and to learn something new. You're not always right, so stop pretending you know everything, and humble yourself to others. If you desire to be listened to, then give others the courtesy of listening to them.

2. **You Should Never Be Too Busy to Listen:** Anyone can add value to your world if you're willing to listen. How many times have you dismissed someone because of a station or title when what you should have done was listen? Wisdom doesn't just come from peers and those above you—it can come from anywhere at any time, but only if you're willing to listen. Expand your sphere of influence and learn from those with different perspectives and experiences—you'll be glad you did.

3. **Listen to Nonverbals:** People say as much (if not more) with their actions, inactions, body language, facial expressions, and so forth, as they do with their verbal communications. Don't be lulled into thinking that because people are not saying something they're not communicating. In fact, most people won't overtly verbalize opposition or disagreement, but they will almost always deliver a very clear message with their nonverbals.

4. **Listen for Opportunity:** Intuitive listeners are looking for the story behind the message, and the opportunity beyond the issue. Listening is about discovery, and discovery doesn't only impact the present, but it can also influence the future.

5. **Let Listening Be Your Calling Card:** One of the best compliments you can be paid is to be known as a good listener. Being recognized in this fashion will open doors, surface opportunities, and take you places that talking never could. Listening demonstrates that you respect others and is the first step in building trust and rapport.

6. **Recognize the Contributions of Others:** One of the most often overlooked aspects of listening is thanking others for their contributions. If you glean benefits from listening to people, thank them. Even if no value is perceived, thank them for their time and input. Never forget to acknowledge those who contribute energy, ideas, actions, or results. Few things go as far in building good will as recognizing others.

Allow me to leave you with one final thought to reflect on—if you're ready for advanced listening skills, don't just listen to those who agree with you, but actively seek out dissenting opinions and thoughts. Listen to those that confront you, challenge you, stretch you, and develop you. True wisdom doesn't see opposition, only opportunity. I believe it was Benjamin Franklin who said, "Speak little, do much." In my opinion great talkers are a dime a dozen, but great listeners are a rare commodity.

Chapter 8

Hacking the Innovation Gap

A lack of innovative thinking is the precursor to a brand in decline.

The need for change exists in every organization. Other than ir-rational change solely for the sake of change, every corporation must change to survive. If your organization doesn't innovate and change in accordance with market-driven needs and demands, it will fail—it's just that simple. Leaders who don't become very skilled at hacking the innovation gap put their organizations on the fast track to obsolescence.

Agility, innovation, disruption, fluidity, decisiveness, commitment, and, above all else, a bias toward action will lead to the creation of innovation and change. It is the implementation of change that results in evolving, growing, and thriving companies. While most executives and entrepreneurs have come to accept the concept of innovation management as a legitimate business practice, and change leadership as a legitimate executive priority in theory, I have found very few organizations that have effectively integrated innovation and change as core disciplines and focus areas in reality.

What's particularly interesting to me is the number of companies who were once dominant brands, based upon their ability to innovate, that ceded their market-leading positions to others when they failed to sustain innovation. There are countless examples of companies throughout history that have either failed to embrace disruptive business models, or have failed to maintain their once disruptive edge.

Let's just take a moment and look at a few notable examples of what happens to companies that become complacent. Why didn't the railroads innovate? Why didn't Folgers recognize the retail consumer demand for coffee and develop a Starbucks-type business model? Why didn't Blockbuster see Netflix coming? Why did traditional learning institutions take so long to move to adaptive online learning? Why did American automakers lose their once-dominant position to their European and Asian counterparts? How did the brick-and-mortar bookstores let Amazon get the jump on them? Why are the cable companies failing to listen to their consumer base and losing market share to innovators like Hulu, Netflix, and other web-based entertainment providers? Is Apple starting to fall into the same trap by allowing other smart phone manufacturers to gain an innovation lead?

I could go on and on with more examples, but the answers to the aforementioned questions are quite simple. The established companies become focused on making incremental gains through process improvements and were satisfied with their business models and didn't even see the innovators coming until it was too late. Their focus shifted from managing opportunities to managing risk, which in turn allowed them to manage themselves into brand decline. They failed to continue hacking innovation.

Hacking the Idea Trap—What Innovation Is Not

It is my hope to help dispel the myth that ideas are inherently good things. Too many companies are long on ideas and short on execution. Too many leaders believe ideas and innovation are one and the same.

Let me be as clear as possible: "Ideas don't equal innovation." In fact, I place little value on ideas. Not only do raw ideas have little intrinsic value, but they are often very costly.

While I stipulate to the fact that ideas can sometimes lead to great things, I also submit that it is more frequently the case that ideas lead to disappointment, and even outright disaster. Those of you familiar with my work are probably wondering if it is really me authoring this text, if you're baffled at how a champion of innovation can simultaneously be an idea basher, I urge you to read on, and I promise the congruity will become apparent.

I want to start by actually defining what an idea is, and is not. Ideas are not a substitute for purpose. Ideas do not constitute a philosophy, principle, or strategy. An idea is not synonymous with a competitive advantage, an idea is not necessarily a sign of creativity, an idea does not constitute innovation, and as much as some people wish it was so, an idea is certainly not a business. To the chagrin of many, ideas in and of themselves are nothing more than unrefined, random thoughts. Ideas on their own accord are really quite useless. The truth can oftentimes be harsh and difficult to hear, but it is nonetheless the truth.

Ideas are a dime a dozen. Take a moment and reflect on all the ideas you've spawned over the years, or the many ideas that have been birthed by your friends, family, and professional associates and you'll quickly see that most of them never got liftoff. The problem is that most ideas never get implemented, and moreover even the best ideas when improperly implemented can cause great harm.

While creativity is clearly a valuable asset, unbridled creativity where random, disparate ideas abound outside of a sound decisioning and execution framework will create distraction and chaos much more often than they will lead to innovation. The difference between an idea and innovation is execution—ideas are ethereal, and innovation adds value. Don't be the "idea" person; be the innovator.

In fact, it is most often the organizations that demonstrate a herd mentality when rushing to adopt the latest ideas that are the farthest thing away from being innovative. The net result of being a late-stage trend follower is that you will likely experience little more than yet another in a long line of great adventures that ended in frustration due to the time wasted and the investment squandered. The reality is that many businesses are quick to recognize great ideas, but they often have no plan for how to successfully integrate them into their business model.

My advice to you is not to let your business get caught up in embracing random ideas—at least not without some initial analysis being conducted to determine the likelihood of success. Failed initiatives are costly at several levels. Aside from being costly, a flawed execution can cast doubt on management credibility, have a negative impact on morale, taint the brand, adversely affect external relationships, and cause a variety of other problems for your business.

The bottom line is that new ideas are beautiful things when they become solutions or lead to opportunities. Properly implemented, capitalizing on process-driven creativity can keep business from stagnating and cause growth and evolution.

Hacking the Change Gap

First the bad news: If you're not willing to embrace change you're not ready to lead. Put simply, leadership is not a static endeavor. In fact, leadership demands fluidity, which requires the willingness to recognize the need for change, and finally, the ability to lead change. Now the good news: As much as some people want to create complexity around the topic of leading change, the reality is that creating, managing, and leading change are all quite simple.

To prove my point, I'll not only explain the entire change life cycle in three short paragraphs, but I'll do it in simple terms anyone can understand. As a bonus I'm also providing you with 10 items to assess in evaluating whether the change you're considering is value added, or just change for the sake of change.

I want to start with offering a brief overview on the topic of change. While there is little debate that the successful implementation of change can create an extreme competitive advantage, it is not well understood that the lack of doing so can send a company (or an individual's career) into a death spiral. Companies that pursue and embrace change are healthy, growing, and dynamic organizations, while companies that fear change are stagnant entities on their way to a slow and painful death.

Agility, innovation, disruption, fluidity, decisiveness, commitment, and above all else, a bias toward action will lead to the creation of change. It is the implementation of change that results in evolving, growing, and thriving companies. As promised, and without further ado, the change life cycle in three easy steps:

1. **Identifying the Need for Change:** The need for change exists in every organization. The most complex area surrounding change is focusing your efforts in the right areas, for the right reasons, and at the right times. The ambiguity and risk can be taken out of the change agenda by simply focusing on three areas: (1) Current Customers—what needs to change to better serve your customers? (2) Potential Customers—what needs to change to profitably create new customers? (3) Corporate Culture—what changes need to occur to better serve your workforce and improve their resources so that they can better influence items one and two above?

2. **Leading Change:** You cannot effectively lead change without understanding the landscape of change. There are four typical responses to change. *The Victim:* Those who view change as a personal attack on their persona, their role, their job, or their area of responsibility. They view everything at an atomic level based upon how they perceive change will directly and indirectly impact them. *The Neutral Bystander:* This group is neither for nor against change. They will not directly or vocally oppose change, nor will they proactively get behind change. The Neutral Bystander will just go with the flow, not wanting to make any waves, and thus hoping to perpetually fly under the radar. *The Critic:* The Critic opposes any and all change. Keep in mind that not all critics are overt in their resistance. Many critics remain in stealth mode trying to derail change behind the scenes by using their influence on others. Whether overt or covert, you must identify critics of change early in the process if you hope to succeed. *The Advocate:* The Advocate not only embraces change, but will evangelize the change initiative. Like the Critics, it is important to identify the Advocates early in the process to not only build the power base for change, but to give momentum and enthusiasm to the change initiative. Once you've identified these change constituencies, you must involve all of them, message

properly to each of them, and don't let up. With the proper messaging and involvement even adversaries can be converted into allies.

3. **Managing Change**: Managing change requires that key players have control over four critical elements: (1) Vision Alignment—those that understand and agree with your vision must be elevated in the change process. Those who disagree must be converted or have their influence neutralized; (2) Responsibility—your change agents must have a sufficient level of responsibility to achieve the necessary results; (3) Accountability—your change agents must be accountable for reaching their objectives; and (4) Authority—if the first three items are in place, yet your change agents have not been given the needed authority to get the job done, the first three items won't mean much. It's critical you set your change agents up for success and not failure by giving them the proper tools, talent, resources, responsibility, and authority necessary for finishing the race.

There you have it; the foundational elements of change in three short paragraphs. Now that you understand change, following are the 10 points that need validating prior to launching a change initiative:

1. **Alignment and Buy-In:** The change being considered should be in alignment with the overall values, vision, and mission of the enterprise. Senior leadership must champion any new initiative. If someone at the C-suite level is against the new initiative, it will likely die a slow and painful death.

2. **Advantage:** If the initiative doesn't provide a unique competitive advantage, preferably a game-changing advantage, it should at least bring you closer to an even playing field.

3. **Value Add:** Any new project should preferably add value to existing initiatives, and if not, it should show a significant enough return on investment to justify the dilutive effect of not keeping the main thing the main thing.

4. **Due Diligence:** Just because an idea sounds good doesn't mean it is. You should endeavor to validate proof of concept based upon detailed, credible research. Do your homework—put the change initiative through a rigorous set of risk/reward and cost/benefit analyses. Forget this step, and you won't be able to find a rock big enough to hide under.

5. **Ease of Use:** Whether the new initiative is intended for your organization, vendors, suppliers, partners, or customers, it must be simple and easy. Usability drives adoptability, and therefore it pays to keep things simple. Don't make the mistake of confusing complexity with sophistication.

6. **Identify the Risks:** Nothing is without risk, and when you think something is without risk, that is when you're most likely to end up in trouble. All initiatives should include detailed risk management provisions that contain sound contingency and exit planning.

7. **Measurement:** Any change initiative should be based upon solid business logic that drives corresponding financial engineering and modeling. Be careful of high-level, pie-in-the-sky projections. The change being adopted must be measurable. Deliverables, benchmarks, deadlines, and success metrics must be incorporated into the plan.

8. **The Project:** Many companies treat change as some ethereal form of management hocus-pocus that will occur by osmosis. A change initiative must be treated as a project. It must be detailed and deliverable on a schedule. The initiative should have a beginning, middle, and end.

9. **Accountability:** Any new initiative should contain accountability provisions. Every task should be assigned and managed according to a plan and in the light of day.

10. **Actionable:** A successful initiative cannot remain in a strategic planning state. It must be actionable through focused tactical implementation. If the change initiative being contemplated is good enough to get through the other nine steps, then it's good enough to execute.

Hacking the Gap between Incremental and Disruptive

By now it should be clear to you that I'm not a huge fan of either/or propositions. In most, if not all cases, decisions that are made on this basis simply constitute a lack of depth and understanding. This particularly holds true as it applies to the topic of innovation methodology. Most innovators view innovation from one of two perspectives: those who believe disruptive innovation is superior to incremental innovation, and those who take the opposite side of the argument. In the text that follows I'll share innovations best kept secret—a different argument altogether.

One of the most popular books in recent years was *Blue Ocean Strategy* by W. Chan Kim and Renée Mauborgne (Harvard Business School Publishing, 2005). The book espouses the benefits of carving out an uncontested market and thereby rendering competition irrelevant. I want to begin by making the argument for incremental innovation; essentially taking the opposite position to Kim and Mauborgne. It is faster, easier, and cheaper to refine something than it is to create it. Let's face it, not all oceans are blue. Even if you find a blue ocean to sail in, there is a lack of certainty as to whether you'll navigate it successfully, and even if you do, as to how long you'll remain the only ship in the ocean. I think most rational people have concluded it is much more profitable to disintermediate a market than it is to build one from scratch.

The main reason attempts at disruptive innovation fail more often than not, and don't happen with more frequency and velocity is that human nature is to make things harder than needed by looking in the wrong places for disruptive opportunities. The real trick, the secret sauce if you will, is to focus on incremental innovation that becomes disruptive. Don't think incremental *versus* disruptive—think incremental *and* disruptive.

This combination of the two practices is the option that allows innovators to have their cake and eat it too. This is what levels the field by bringing disruptive opportunities in reach of companies that don't have the time or resources to create new markets.

Let me be as clear as I can—disruptive innovation isn't limited to a sole focus on creation of something new. Disruption can occur by disintermediating, refining, reengineering, or optimizing a product/service, role/function/practice, category, market, sector, or industry. The most successful companies combine disruptive thinking with incremental approaches in order to manage risk, gain time-to-market advantages, add value to core initiatives, and leverage built-in efficiencies and economies of scale.

The problem with most incremental approaches to innovation is that companies don't think big enough. Most incremental approaches more closely resemble process engineering/automation efforts with a focus on cost reduction through gaining efficiency, not on revenue creation by causing disruption. Removing self-imposed restrictions on thinking will result in opening up more opportunities to innovate around.

The good news is this: There's an easy fix to this antiquated way of thinking, which is currently crippling the innovation efforts of many companies, and it's found by adhering to the following six-step process:

1. **Define:** The first thing that needs to happen is to define what constitutes disruption. Set a standard and then stick to it. I'm not suggesting that any initiative not meeting the definition be halted, but I am suggesting that you not fool yourself and label something as disruptive when it is clearly not.

2. **Identify:** Now that you've defined what types of projects you're looking for, aggressively begin pursuing projects that meet the standards.

3. **Assess:** Once a potential project has been identified, put it under intense scrutiny and understand what you're dealing with before you pull the trigger. Based upon the standards that were set in the definition phase, create a scoring/ranking system based on key metrics and prioritize initiatives accordingly.

4. **Plan:** Be strategic. Great outcomes rarely occur when initiatives are under-resourced and/or poorly led. Deploy your best resources against your greatest opportunities. Make sure you set projects up for success rather than failure.

5. **Implement:** Get tactical. The best strategies will end up facing certain failure unless planning transitions into practice. Without prudent, decisive, consistent, and productive forward progress, plans aren't worth the paper they're written on. Planning without implementation is an exercise in frivolity.

6. **Monitor:** Everything in business, including the best laid plans, is subject to changes in circumstances and market conditions. Put simply, static plans are bad plans. Make sure that all efforts are measured against milestones, benchmarks, deadlines, budgets, and so forth. If the plan needs to be nuanced in order to achieve success, then have the flexibility engineered into your plan to allow for needed changes.

Hacking the Next Level

At one time or another all great leaders experience something so big and so impactful it changes the landscape—it's what I call a *game changer*. A game changer is that ah-ha moment where you see something others don't. It's the transformational magic that takes organizations from ordinary to exceptional. In the text that follows I'll provide you with a blue print for manufacturing ah-ha moments.

I've mentioned pursuit in more than a few places throughout this book. If you've ever wondered how people come up with the proverbial *big idea*—wonder no more. The answer is found in relentless pursuit—they work at it. Put simply, the best leaders proactively focus on pursing game changers. They're never satisfied with the ordinary or mundane.

Elon Musk, Richard Branson, Jeff Bezos, Dick Costolo, Larry Page, and other CEOs recognized for their big ideas didn't just get lucky—they were/are committed to the constant pursuit of game changers. They aren't just dreamers—they are doers. Successful leaders are nothing if not persistent, committed individuals who understand potential is of little value if said potential fails to be realized.

One of the things wrong with today's marketplace is there's far too much rehashing of old ideas spun as new. Great leaders aren't copycats—they abhor *me too* business methodologies. Leaders who pursue game changers have no patience for the status quo—they focus their efforts on shattering the status quo. Game changers refuse to allow their organizations to adopt conventional orthodoxy and bureaucracy—they challenge norms, break conventions, and encourage diversity of thought. The message here is a simple one—don't copy, create. Don't just play the game—change the game. The goals are to create, improve on, and innovate around *best* practices in order to find *next* practices.

Leaders who create or inspire game changers are nothing if not aware. Not only are they self-aware, they're aware of the emotions and needs of others, and they are also clearly aware of what will be embraced in the market. They possess a refined blend of intrinsic curiosity and extrinsic focus. Perhaps most of all, game-changing leaders are in touch with a greater purpose—they understand the value of serving something beyond themselves.

Take the qualities I've mentioned above and apply them to the following framework and you'll find ah-ha moments a bit easier to come by. The following six steps represent my personal process for finding and implementing game changers—I call it SMARTS? (**S**imple-**M**eaningful-**A**ctionable-**R**elational-**T**ransformational-**S**calable):

1. **S**imple—While not all game changers are simple, the best ones usually are. It was Albert Einstein who said, *If you can't explain it simply, you don't understand it well enough.* In most cases, simple can be translated as realistic, cost effective, quick to adopt, and fast to implement. Don't get entangled in complexities—become heavily invested in simplicity.

2. **M**eaningful—Game changers have great purpose, meet a need, solve a problem, serve an existing market, or create a new one—they are meaningful. Most leaders get sucked down into the weeds and spend too much of their valuable time majoring in the minors. If it's not really meaningful, if it doesn't serve a greater purpose, if it's not a game changer, why do it? Ideas, products, services, and/or solutions that focus on value creation fare better than those that don't.

3. **A**ctionable—It's not a game changer if whatever "it" is never gets off the drawing board. If you cannot turn an idea into innovation, if you can't put thought into practice, then it's not a game changer. By definition game changers happen, they exist, they have life. They don't lurk in the shadowlands of the ethereal and esoteric, they become reality.

4. **R**elational—I have found game changers enhance, extend, and leverage existing relationships, as well as serve to create new ones. When you get down to brass tacks, all business boils down to people (employees, customers, partners, investors, vendors, etc.), and people mean relationships. Real game changers understand the power of people and relationships, and they embody this in both their construction and implementation. If you forget the people, you cannot have a game changer.

5. **T**ransformational—I have yet to see a static game changer. By definition, a game changer causes change. If nothing changes, if nothing is created, if nothing is improved, if nothing is transformed, then you don't have a game changer. A lesson that I learned long ago is that you simply cannot experience sustainable improvement without transformation.

6. **S**calable—If it's not scalable, it's not a game changer. An idea that offers no hope of a future will more often than not turn into a

nightmare rather than fulfill a dream. True game changers are built with velocity and sustainability in mind. The best thing about real games changers is they build upon themselves to catalyze other accretive opportunities.

So there you have it—now that I've shared my thoughts on creating game changers, my SMARTS if you will, it's your turn to go out and create a few game changers.

Hacking the Competition

Competition is to be feared only if it is not understood. If understood, competition is not only healthy, it can also be very prosperous. If you really want to understand leaders' perspective on the market, ask them about their competition.

Leaders' views on competition will not only reveal a lot about their beliefs on current and future market trends, but also on innovation, branding, talent management, supply chain issues, constituency management, capital markets, and customer facing. Whether you want to admit it or not, competition is part of your world, and likely a bigger part than you'd care to admit.

Every leader has an approach to dealing with competition. Some leaders completely ignore the topic of competition as if it doesn't exist, others view competition as a minor nuisance; some executives see the competitive landscape as a battlefield where war is waged on a daily basis, and others view competition as untapped opportunities for collaboration and innovation. Smart leaders are fluid in their approach and understand that competition can breed significant opportunity.

I'm always amazed by those who regard the topic of competition as simplistic, not relevant, or sophomoric. They tend to dismiss this subject as if it somehow diminishes their business savvy to admit they have competition. These captains of their own destiny share the perspective that competition is not a significant factor in the execution of their business plan—they're in control, and competition is irrelevant. While this may make for a nice sound bite, I don't buy it, and if they're truly honest with themselves, neither do they. In business, you can either choose to deal with your competition (even if that means partnering with them), or you can opt to stand idly by and let the competition eat your lunch.

While some companies talk a good game with regard to competitive strategy, in my experience very few businesses actually address the issue in adequate fashion. I suppose much of my perspective on competition was formed during my days as a soldier and athlete. In the military, we valued actionable intelligence, studied our enemy's strengths and weaknesses, developed a battle plan around a solid strategy, and executed our tactical mission as if our lives depended on it—because they did.

Similarly, in my days as an athlete (long, long ago), our game plan each week was refined based upon the strengths and weaknesses of the team we were playing next. If we didn't study films and scouting reports, develop plays that would exploit match-ups, and execute our game plan, we would lose—it was as simple as that.

Dealing with competition in the business world is really no different from dealing with enemies on the battlefield or competitors on the athletic field . . . you either win or lose based upon your state of preparedness, perspective, interpretation, and execution. In the following two paragraphs I share my views on competition so that you can understand how I personally navigate this issue.

There is arguably no more competitive space than what exists in the professional services arena. While I tend to view my competition as peers and colleagues, it is not lost on me that my clients have a choice. The client is in control. Not me, nor my competitor—the client. I know who my competition is, and I know where and when I'm a better choice. I have a very strong understanding of where I can create the most value for my clients. Where I'm not the best fit, I refer my peers, or in some cases I partner with them, but I attempt to ensure that the client receives the best solution whether or not said solution includes me or my firm.

Put simply, I deal with competition by attempting to create the best solution for my clients. Sometimes this includes my colleagues, and sometimes it excludes them. One final thought here—the competition I'm most concerned about is not the competition that I know, but the competition that I don't. I'm always on the lookout for new practitioners entering the market where we have practice areas, disruptive technology, or changes in the landscape that could disintermediate certain aspects of the market. I worry much more about the unknown than the known.

Now it's your turn—how well do you know your competition? No really—not how well do you think you know your competition, but how well do you really understand them? I've often found executives when asked about their competition tend to talk about the organization that most closely resembles their own. That's nice, but how much time do you spend evaluating people, entities, or technology that may not be competition presently, but could be down the road? Do you have a business intelligence platform? When was the last time you conducted a formal competitive study? Do your R&D and innovation programs evaluate the competitive landscape? Do your marketing, PR, and branding initiatives satisfactorily address the competition? Do you stack up as well as you think, or have you just adopted a position out of convenience?

The first step in developing a competitive strategy is to identify your current and potential threats, and then to prioritize said threats based upon perceived risk/reward and cost/benefit scenarios. The following list is clearly not exhaustive, but it is representative of the main competitive threats to a business. Competition can come in the form of any one or combination of the following 10 potential threats:

1. Existing or potential direct and indirect competitors.
2. Existing clients or end users that could either become competition or strengthen your competitors if they have a change in loyalty.
3. Current or former employees who could become competition.
4. Vendors, suppliers, or distributors that could become competition or provide an edge to your competition.
5. Competitive innovations in process, management, talent, pricing, efficiency, and so on that can cause disruption in the market.
6. Strong changes in brand perception via news, PR, branding, litigation and so on can create changes in the competitive landscape.
7. Competitive technology innovations that could adversely impact your business.
8. Competitive mergers, acquisitions, and roll-ups that could adversely impact your business.
9. Political, legislative, regulatory, or compliance actions that could create a competitive imbalance in the market.
10. Changes in general market dynamics that could create competitive changes in the market.

Once all areas of competitive risk have been identified and prioritized, it will be much easier to develop a strategy for stacking the odds in your favor, regardless of when, where, or how you encounter the competition. The key to successfully exploiting competition over the long haul is linking your competitive strategy to the discipline of innovation and the mind-set of being externally focused with regard to the market.

While customer centricity is important, don't forget to look for new customers/markets as well. Maintaining your existing revenue base is important, but deepening and expanding relationships is even more important. A sustainable competitive advantage is not found by creating minor advantages in product features. Long-term advantages are created by innovating around the needs of the market with a focus on sustainable value creation.

Hacking the Flexibility Gap

Of the many things I took away from my time in the military two statements remain top of mind: "adapt, improvise, and overcome" and "prior proper planning prevents poor performance." The military not only develops its leaders to be prepared, but also for how to deal with unexpected change rapidly thrust upon them. People who have spent time in the military have learned how to be very fluid in the execution of their duties—they are nothing if not capable of real-time flexibility.

In addition to working with clients who possess great leadership acumen, I have the privilege of working with some truly amazing leadership talent at my firm. In fact, one of the most gifted and humble leaders I've ever had the pleasure of working with is Brian Layer, brigadier general, United States Army (retired). Brian knows a few things about leadership. Brian is a West Point graduate who also holds three masters degrees. He twice commanded a brigade in Iraq, and I'm proud to say Brian now chairs our organizational development practice at N2growth.

A particular area of focus for Brian is helping organizations, teams, and leaders to become more creative and flexible in how they adapt to changing circumstances. One of the ways Brian's organization accomplishes this is by borrowing a practice from the military known as *red teaming*. This is a process for conducting extremely effective threat/vulnerability assessments and then developing rapid action plans to eliminate the heretofore-unrecognized risk and/or to create new-found opportunity.

Whether we provide red teaming as an outside assessment or help organizations to form their own red teaming initiative, the goal is not just to create an exercise, but to embed a disruptive ethos into how an organization views itself from the inside out and outside in. The fundamental precept of red teaming is to challenge institutional thinking, dominant logic, and current practices for the purpose of developing better options for decision making leading to better outcomes.

In other words, the purpose of red teaming is to develop a framework for challenging the status quo in order to create strategic and operational advantage in current and future environments. It forces an organization to gut-check itself and to creatively seek innovation where it will have the biggest impact. The red teaming practice has been invaluable to our military's success in recent years. While somewhat new in business circles, we believe corporations will receive the same value from subjecting themselves to the challenge and rigor of red teaming.

The whole purpose of giving you a brief look inside the world of red teaming is to illustrate that the best organizations are constantly looking to become faster and more aggressive in seeking out change that creates an advantage. So-called *deep-dives*, *strategy refreshes*, *lean initiatives*, and other typical corporate planning initiatives, while useful to an extent, aren't nearly as thorough and/or effective as they need to be.

What are you doing now that is different from what you've done before? What are you doing today that challenges the very construct of how and why decisions are made? The simple truth of the matter is that most businesses are not fully aware of the risks they face or the opportunities they're missing—it remains business as usual.

While the benefits of red teaming are almost too numerous to mention, even if you fail to implement this standard of challenge, you need to move as close to it as you can get. Leadership is nothing if not flexible, contextual, and ever seeking positive change and growth. How open are you and your organization to the possibility of a new and better way? Chances are your self-proclaimed on-time airline isn't as on-time as you'd like to believe.

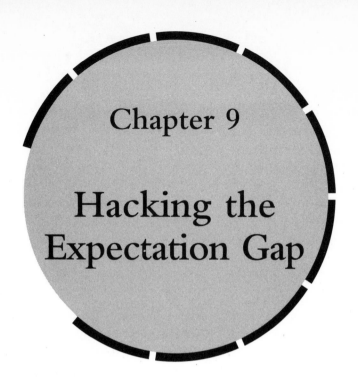

Chapter 9

Hacking the
Expectation Gap

Managing expectations is gamesmanship—
aligning them is leadership.

This is perhaps the shortest chapter in the book, but it is also one of the most important. Few things harm the forward progress of an organization like leaders who fail to understand the value of aligning expectations. What leaders say, how they say it, and whether or not they follow through on what they say matters greatly.

Leaders can overcome many mistakes, but rarely can they overcome a loss of trust and credibility stemming from a failure to keep their commitments. Equally as difficult to overcome is a gap in trust that occurs when leaders ask for one thing, but hold people accountable for something altogether different from what they asked for.

Hacking the Alignment Gap

When it comes to leadership, I can share the issues of creating and delivering *expectations* are no small matter. In fact, understanding how to come out on the right side of the expectation curve can often be the difference between being viewed as an average leader and one held in high regard.

Moving the goal posts by arbitrarily raising and lowering expectations creates confusion, and is often an intellectually dishonest exercise. Aligning expectations doesn't need to be difficult—set them, align them, stick to them, and execute on them. Attempting to lead without an understanding of how to hack the expectation gap is simply an exercise in frivolity.

Conflicts, disagreements, disputes, and litigation are often born out of expectation gaps. The thing leaders need to keep in mind is expectations cut both ways. Keeping what you perceive as being your end of the bargain is only half of the equation, as what you think only matters if it's in alignment with the understanding of the other party.

We have all found ourselves in the unenviable position of assigning work product only to end up with the deliverable falling far short of expectations, while having the producers of said work product thinking they exceeded all expectations. I've often said that those leaders who fail to clearly communicate their expectations have no right to them.

Nothing engenders confidence and creates a trust bond like delivering on promises made, and, likewise, few things erode confidence and credibility like commitments not kept. Leaders who deliver on promises quickly rise to the top, and those that fail to develop this skill won't survive long. The best leaders make a practice of saying what they mean, meaning what they say, and doing what they say they'll do.

The science of aligning expectations is about systematically connecting what is said with what is done. The art of aligning expectations is about closing, or better yet, eliminating the expectation gap. Blend the art and science together and you have the framework for what is becoming the differentiating factor in performance-based decisioning.

The truth of the matter is leadership is very, very hard—but it's not overly complex. That said, weak leaders tend to overcomplicate everything they touch. At its core, leadership is as simple as setting the expectation with clear and crisp communication, aligning any gaps in expectations, and then rallying the right talent around the delivery of the shared expectation.

Most of the challenges businesses and their leaders encounter are born out of broken promises, misaligned commitments, or poorly structured agreements. I have always believed that promises made are somewhat meaningless, but promises kept are invaluable. Furthermore, I've found the easiest way to judge a leader is by balancing the scorecard between promises made and promises kept.

Several years ago I created the Venn diagram depicted in Figure 9.1 to explain the confluence of factors that need to occur in order to close the expectation gap.

Expectations exist throughout the entire value chain, with all stakeholders needing and deserving to have their expectations understood and met (hopefully exceeded). Whether it is addressing customer expectations, board expectations, shareholder or analyst expectations, or the inverse situation of employees having to deal with the expectations of executives, it is the ability to excel at decisioning based upon setting, aligning, and executing expectations that creates high-performance organizations.

Promises made and consistently kept, based upon solid reasoning and underlying business logic, will help to create a solid brand attracting loyal customers and talented employees. The following three practices will help create an organization that delivers on its commitments:

1. **Collaborate Early and Often:** Decisioning in a vacuum, or without all the facts, will place you in a deficit from the beginning.

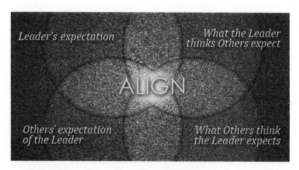

Figure 9.1   Confluence of Factors Needed to Occur to Close the Expectation Gap

It is at best extremely difficult to align expectations and deliver on commitments made if you don't have clear visibility as to what is wanted or needed. Before making promises or commitments, collaborate with all concerned parties to ensure that expectations are understood.

2. **Resist Making Verbal Commitments:** Most misunderstandings occur as a result of improper interpretation of oral communications. Most broken commitments result from impulsive verbal promises made before all the details were sorted out. Once you have gained clarity as to the perceived need to be fulfilled, place your understanding of the deliverables in writing by outlining key business points and circulate the document for review and comments. Where possible, resist formalizing agreements, proposals, or other commitments until you have alignment on key expectations and deliverables.

3. **Treat Promises Like Projects:** Build a culture that breaks down all commitments into deliverables, benchmarks, and deadlines. Allocate resources, budget, and staff while delivering the commitment within a framework of measured accountability. Treating all commitments and promises as formal projects will help manage performance risk and will also create continuity of process and delivery.

Performance-focused decisioning based upon principles of expectation alignment will lead to a certainty of execution that should translate into one of your company's greatest competitive advantages. The best leaders recognize they can promise and deliver, underpromise and overdeliver, or even overpromise and deliver . . . they just don't dare overpromise and underdeliver.

Hacking the Discipline Gap

One of the fastest ways to ensure that expectations will fail to become aligned is to lack discipline. The difference between good and great often comes down to discipline. So my question is this—how disciplined are you as a leader? Context, fluidity, and other nuanced behaviors are positive traits to embrace so long as they don't serve as an excuse for a lack of discipline.

I'm not suggesting that leaders should be robotic or static in approach—quite the contrary. Implementing a framework of discipline allows leaders more flexibility not less. While subjecting yourself to the rigor of discipline is not easy, it is essential if you want to maximize your effectiveness as a leader.

It's simply impossible to consistently communicate and align expectations when you're always shooting from the hip. The best leaders I know are extremely disciplined people—they simply do the things others are not willing to do. They are disciplined enough to be willing to seek understanding and alignment prior to pushing for the solution. Are you disciplined in all facets of your life, or just those that come more easily to you?

There's a lot of material in circulation about strengths and weaknesses, but the truth of the matter is the mantra of *playing to your strengths* is often an excuse to avoid doing things you dislike or don't happen to be very good at. The truth of the matter is that it's much easier for most people to refine their areas of giftedness and revel in the admiration of being a high achiever than it is to be honest about their shortcomings.

I want you to take a hard look in the mirror—is it truly an attempt to increase your efficiency that guides you to play to your strengths, or is it pride, ego, arrogance, and laziness that preclude you from being disciplined? Remember that being efficient is not always the same thing as being effective. Here's the thing—you don't need to observe leaders for long to know whether or not they're disciplined. Disciplined leaders stand out because they're the ones that get things done—the ones you can count on.

How many times have you put up with, or overlooked certain weaknesses in people because of their considerable strengths in other areas? Wouldn't it be better to find yourself in a place where others weren't tolerating certain of your behaviors in lieu of others? It's been said, "Discipline is the refining fire by which talent becomes ability." Wouldn't it be better to be viewed as a complete package—the real deal? Sure it would, so why not apply the discipline it takes to ensure that outcome?

I want you to envision a golfer who is long off the tee—the grip it and rip it type who can outdrive anyone on the range, yet never wins a round because of a pathetic short game. Here's the thing: It's not that these champions of the long drive can't master the short game—they just spend more time on the driving range than on the putting green. They would rather receive the accolades that are sure to come from their mighty display in the tee box rather than suffer the chuckles that might result from sculling a chip shot around the putting green. Know the type? The sad thing is they don't just exist on the golf course.

My bottom line is this: Real leaders strive for complete align-ment—they constantly seek improvement. If you want to become a true standout, as opposed to someone who has great potential, my mes-sage is simple—become very intentional about bringing discipline and rigor to every area of your life. Take an assessment of what you do well and what you don't, and then apply structure and discipline to each of those areas. Hard work isn't easy, but reaching a true point of alignment where everyone is singing off the same proverbial sheet of music pays huge dividends.

The truly great leaders seek out gaps in alignment and close them—do you?

Chapter 10

Hacking the Complexity Gap

Complexity is the enemy of the productive—it stifles creativity, slows progress, increases costs, inhibits confidence, and erodes culture.

I want you to put on your consumer hat for a moment and answer this question: What do you do when you encounter complexity as part of the purchasing process? If you're anything like me, you disengage and look to make your purchase elsewhere. What do you do when you experience complexity in the service arena? Again, if you're anything like me you look for another company to service your business.

When it comes to business and leadership, complexity is never your friend. There's an old saying in the software business that *usability drives adoptability*—it's not just true in the software business. I don't know anyone who doesn't prefer simplicity to complexity. Have you ever had a question, issue, or concern and needed to contact a company only to find out they don't even list a phone number? Does it matter to you that as a paying customer that company has gone out of their way not to talk to you?

It is almost as if business people have come to believe that complexity is synonymous with sophistication and savvy. It has been my experience that the only things that "complexity" is synonymous with are increased costs and failed implementations. Complexity is precisely what plagues many businesses.

You don't solve complicated matters by adding to the complexity. The most effective way to deal with complexity is to strip it away through refining efforts rooted in simplicity. Leaders must become highly skilled at hacking complexity if they hope to build effective organizations.

I've left the following challenge open for years for any company who wants to take me up on it: I guarantee I can walk into any business and within 90 days eliminate a minimum of 20 percent of their existing processes, rules, policies, and procedures resulting in increased gains in performance, morale, effectiveness, and a substantial lowering of costs. I've actually done this countless times and have yet to fail. Virtually every business suffers from being overmatrixed, oversiloed, overprocessed, and overmanaged.

All businesses can benefit from a focus on simplicity. The truth of the matter is most businesses have too many people and too many resources focused on things that don't matter. There are too many people in leadership positions who spend their time justifying insanity rather than attempting to vanquish it.

Hacking Complexity

Simplifying something doesn't make it a trite or incomplete endeavor. Simplification makes for a more productive and efficient effort that is often more savvy than other, more complex alternatives. Another benefit of simplicity is that it serves as a key driver of focus, which enables greater efficiency, productivity, and better overall performance.

Keeping things simple allows you to focus on one thing at a time without the distractions that complexity breeds by its nature alone. I would suggest that you break down every key area of your business (operations, administration, marketing, branding, sales, finance, IT, etc.) and attempt to simplify your processes, initiatives, and offerings.

One of the most effective ways to order your world is to simplify everything you encounter. However, the problem for many is keeping it simple often becomes very difficult when our basic human nature is to overcomplicate everything we touch. In thinking about the people I respect the most, to the one, they possess the uncanny ability to take the most complicated of issues and simplify them. You will find that the best leaders, communicators, teachers, innovators, and so on have a true knack for taking extremely complex, dense, or intricate content and making it engaging and easy to understand. In fact, it was Leonardo da Vinci who said: "simplicity is the ultimate form of sophistication."

While simplicity may have become a lost art, understanding the importance of simplicity is nonetheless critical to your success. Consider all the presentations/meetings you've attended in the last few weeks; was it the people who were able to articulate their positions in a simple and straightforward fashion, or the individuals that made things complex and tedious that got traction with their ideas? It has been my experience that the more complicated, difficult, or convoluted an explanation is, the more likely it is that one or both of the following issues is at play: (1) the person speaking is a horrible communicator, or (2) the person speaking really doesn't possess a true command of their subject matter. It is one thing to toss around the latest buzzwords or to have the most complex flow chart, but it is quite another thing to actually possess such a deep and thorough understanding of your topic that you can make even the most complex issues easy to understand.

Hacking Smart

Business people are smart people, and smart people like smart things. We have become accustomed to smartphones, smart cards, smart cars, smart homes, and so on, but when it comes to business, what we really need is fewer smart businesses. In fact, I'd say what we really need are more dumb businesses. I know that might sound strange, but stick with me, and I'll explain why I believe dumb is the new smart.

How dumb is your business? At the risk of drawing the ire of corporate elitists, I submit to you that the dumber your business is, the better off you are. The truth is that great companies are those that can thrive and prosper in the absence of complexity and sophistication. As odd as it sounds, businesses that are not dependent on smart talent, capital, or technology can scale faster and easier than those businesses burdened with the aforementioned dependencies.

The simple truth of the matter is that if your business requires smart money (which equals expensive money), or your competitive advantage is tied to superhero key employees, or your business is built around maintaining a technology advantage, you have more weakness in your business model than you do strengths.

Let's drill down on the talent argument a bit deeper. I'm not suggesting for a moment that you don't want to hire tier-one talent. However, I am clearly stating that you don't want to be dependent upon tier-one talent. Talent is clearly a plus as long as it is a value-add and not a business requirement.

If your company's long-term business plan requires the acquisition, or retention of the über employee, then your business not only has a risk-management issue, but it is likely not scalable. If mere mortals can't operate your company, you need to reexamine your business logic. Here is a simple rule of thumb, the bigger the key man policy, or the larger the signing bonus, the less scalable the company is.

The dumb factor not only applies to talent, capital, and technology, but it also extends throughout the entire value chain. It applies to your branding, marketing, supply chain, and ultimately to your customer base. If your customer has to be a rocket scientist to understand your value proposition, you have problems. If your employees cannot simply and effectively explain what you do, you have problems.

The last point I want to cover is that of growth as it relates to dumb businesses. Both scalable and nonscalable businesses can achieve growth and sustainable success. However, it is important to understand the distinction between the two. While a business cannot scale without growth, a business can grow without being scalable. If your business model requires implicit customer growth, your business might grow for a time period certain, but it isn't scalable.

Let me offer a case study in the value of simplicity. Unilever is one of my favorite companies on the planet. They have over 400 brands, sold in more than 190 countries, and Unilever does in excess of €51 billion in annual revenue. More than 170,000 people work for Unilever, and on any given day, more than 2 billion consumers around the world use their products.

While I could talk about Unilever's innovative approach to doing business locally on a global scale, their commitment to purpose and sustainability, their thought leadership, or their progressive business model, it's their commitment to simplicity that I want to highlight.

If any company has a reason to accept complexity, it would be Unilever, but they are in fact committed to simplicity. After decades of M&A activity, Unilever found their brand portfolio has mushroomed to more than 1,200 assets. Unlike some companies that would wear this as a badge of honor, Unilever saw it as a distraction and dilutive to their core focus.

With a focus on simplification, Unilever was not only able to shrink their portfolio from 1,200 brands down to 400, but their sales, revenue, and profit all increased. The company's leadership can now focus efforts on the most meaningful products and markets and not suffer the burden of managing unnecessary and unprofitable complexity.

It's been said there is nothing simple about the practice of simplicity. The reality is it's much easier to allow complexity to set in than it is to continue to strive for simplicity. But whether it's the simplicity of Unilever's brand strategy, buying a pair of shoes from Zappos, using the search interface on Google, or downloading an app to your iPhone, simplicity matters. It matters to the consumer, it matters to your workforce, and it matters to the growth and the sustainability of your enterprise.

The moral of this story is that while sophistication and complexity often go hand-in-hand, they don't have to be synonymous.

Chapter 11

Hacking the Failure Gap

The only real leadership failure is failing to focus on the main thing—serving those you lead. Everything else is merely a development opportunity.

Fear and *failure* are *not* dirty words, but you'll find most leaders treat them as such. They go out of their way to hide their fears and explain away their failures rather than confront them and learn from them. One of my pet peeves is the current trend of labeling fear as a weakness and failure as unacceptable. Leaders must understand how to give permission to fail in a way that moves things forward not sets them back. Understanding how to hack the failure gap empowers your team to think and act differently—a good thing.

Fear in and of itself is not a bad thing, rather it is how people choose to cope with fear that will determine its effect on their life. Ask people who have been in combat, and they'll tell you that it is their innate and often heightened sense of fear that helped to keep them alive. Good soldiers don't give into fear, but they learn to respect and manage their fear so that it actually becomes their ally and not their adversary.

Show me someone who fears nothing, and I'll show you someone who lacks judgment. Show me someone who has fears but refuses to admit them, and I'll show you someone who has an issue with pride and arrogance. Fear doesn't make you weak, nor does it mean that you lack faith or ability, it just means you're human. I learned long ago that fear is a warning sign that needs not to be ignored or hidden, but understood and addressed. I have fears and so do you, so why not bring them out into the light of day and deal with them. Trust me when I tell you that you'll be better off for doing so—I am.

So, what's the greatest fear possessed by leaders? It has been my experience that the greatest fear most professionals struggle with is the fear of failure. In fact, it is oftentimes this *fear of failure* that governs how much risk business people will take, and in turn how successful (or not) they are likely to become.

The same principles discussed above with regard to dealing with your fears also apply to topic of failure. Everyone reading this book has failed, and I hate to break it to you, but you're going to have more failures in your future. Life will become much easier to navigate when you learn to accept failure as healthy and normal. From my perspective, when my life is void of failures, I'm not growing, developing, stretching, or pushing. Put simply, if I'm not failing, then I'm not trying. I've experienced lots of failures, and I'm better for them.

Most professionals don't naturally associate the words "success" and "failure" as having anything to do with one another. However under the right circumstances, failure is absolutely the best experiential learning tool available. Furthermore, I would go so far as to say failure is an essential element of becoming successful. In fact, if you show me a professional who has never experienced failure, I'll say that professional either hasn't tried hard enough or is very new to the world of business.

Hacking Perfection

This may be difficult for some to get their heads around, but perfectionism is *not* a leadership trait. Leadership requires attention to detail and a commitment to quality, but rarely does it require perfection. While leadership doesn't require being perfect, it does require doing what is needed and necessary. Perhaps one of the biggest flaws with the concept of perfection is found in who defines perfect—the definition of perfection will almost always vary radically from person to person. In the text that follows, I'll share my thoughts on the *myth* of perfection.

General George S. Patton said it best: "A good plan violently executed today is far and away better than a perfect plan tomorrow." The pursuit of perfection is one of great adversaries of speed, performance, and execution. In fact, at the risk of being controversial I'm going to take the position that perfection does not exist. I hate to break it to you, but those of you who regard yourselves as perfectionists simply exhibit perfectionistic tendencies in an unrealistic attempt to achieve what cannot be had.

News Flash: speed trumps perfectionism. Perfectionists tend to be very busy, but rarely are they productive. Moreover, the pursuit of perfectionism rarely results in a competitive advantage, but it will result in time delays, cost overruns, missed deadlines, and unkept commitments. I would suggest that rather than seeking what cannot in most cases ever be achieved, that it makes more sense to seek the highest standard of quality that can be delivered in the shortest period of time, and that is economically balanced relative to the constraints of an ever-shifting marketplace.

A huge problem for leaders who regard themselves as perfectionists is that they often set the bar so high that others feel as if they cannot ever meet expectations. As a leader, if you find yourself always wondering, "why others just don't seem to get it," then you likely don't value the contributions of others as much as you desire others to adopt your thinking. Leaders who fall prey to perfectionism tend to focus on the negatives, having a hard time looking past perceived weaknesses to find strengths. The downside of this is that it stifles candor, creativity, and innovation and often leads to a "my way or the highway" environment.

Here's another pet peeve—the phrase "would you rather have something quick or right" makes me cringe every time I hear it. It is one of the most common copouts inept leaders use in masking their decisioning inadequacies. It's as if using this phrase somehow justifies delaying pronouncement on the grounds that they currently possess insufficient information to make an astute decision. Almost without fail, this tactic is a trite and clichéd attempt to somehow insinuate that speed in decisioning is a weakness, and that quick decisions are somehow synonymous with reckless decisions. I would caution you against confusing speed with reckless abandon. I'm a big proponent of planning, assessment, analysis, and strategy, but only if it is concluded in a timely fashion. Analysis paralysis leads to missed opportunities and failed initiatives. Speed is your friend. Embrace it. Leverage it. Win with it.

Time to face the facts: We live in a digital world where the speed of engagement, response, interaction, communication, delivery, and so forth was once a unique competitive value proposition. It is now a requirement for survival. As a leader you must quickly be able to assess risk and make timely decisions.

Put simply, leaders cannot be successful being guided by fear and hesitation. I can tell you that without question the best leaders are able to make very complex decisions, on short time frames, and with incomplete information. If you don't possess the experience or intellectual acuity to make quick decisions that are also good decisions, then you had better surround yourself with sound counsel and advice from those who can.

While there is little debate that speed can create an extreme competitive advantage, it is not well understood that the lack of speed can send a company (or a career) into a death spiral. Agility, fluidity, decisiveness, commitment, and focus all lead to the creation of speed that results in a certainty of execution. There is great truth in the old saying "the best decision is a quick decision, the next best decision is no decision, and the worst decision is a slow decision."

Hacking a Defensive Mind-set

While most of my references to Apple thus far have been as an example of excellence, their perfectionistic tendencies and noncompetitive versioning cycles are putting them at risk. Let me contrast Google and Apple as they relate to the topic at hand.

Google and Apple are both highly esteemed brands. Both companies share many common traits that have contributed to their success, but there is one very big difference between the two—Google plays offense while Apple has recently settled for playing defense. Apple is struggling to maintain its position in the market, while Google is expanding its position.

Fact: even the best defense in the world can't win a game if the offense doesn't put some points on the scoreboard. Think about any organization that devolved from exceptional to good, good to mediocre, or good to gone and you'll find they all share one thing in common—they started playing defense when they should have been playing offense.

Google could have made the decision to stay solely focused on search, but they had the foresight to move beyond the certainty of *what is* to pursue new opportunity by focusing on *what if*. Sure, Google has maintained their position as the dominant search platform (by playing offense), but they have also leveraged their offensive mind-set to exert dominance in categories outside of search as well.

Apple on the other hand, while once the leading innovator in the smartphone space, has ceded that position to other more aggressive players like Samsung, HTC, and yes, Google. Where Apple went wrong is that they began to confuse version releases and feature improvements with innovation. What Apple is learning the hard way is that even the most loyal base of consumers will jump ship when provided a valid reason to do so.

To create something of value is a significant accomplishment. However, the concept many fail to grasp is that value creation is only sustainable if it continues to be scalable. Think of it like this—the only way to protect value is to create more of it. The minute value stands still is the very minute the market adapts and your competition will begin to erode the value you worked so hard to create.

Think of any great brand during its heyday, and you'll find that its owners defended it by playing very aggressive offense. They were in constant growth mode fueled by purpose-driven innovation. They did not settle for protecting what they had created, but put everything they had into innovating beyond their creation. Put simply, a lack of innovative thinking is the precursor to a brand in decline.

Examine any category leaders, and you'll quickly realize what put them at the head of the class to begin with—leadership who valued innovation, and all the good things it affords (healthy culture, ability to attract and retain talent, a focus on the consumer, and alignment to a cohesive vision). When companies begin to overemphasize risk management, and deemphasize opportunity management, the nauseous stench of status quo will begin wafting through the enterprise in epidemic proportion.

The best leaders understand that *usual* and *customary* are not necessarily synonymous with *healthy* and *thriving*. The real key to innovative thinking begins with an open mind—recognition that those who think differently aren't inferior, nor are they a threat. An open mind is a sign of confidence, which allows leaders to recognize diversity of opinion leads to better thinking, better discovery, and better outcomes.

My bottom line is this: If you wear perfectionism as a badge of honor, it is time for a shift in thinking. Others won't see it as a badge of honor, but as a sign of pride, ego, arrogance, or ignorance.

Hacking Succession

Tackling the top of failure without discussing the critical nature of succession would constitute leadership negligence. Succession is a very real concern for every organization—or at least it should be. The thing every leader needs to understand is that when it comes to succession, it's not a matter of *if* but *when*. No leader can lead forever. Failing to plan for the inevitable is irresponsible, but failing to execute the plan is tantamount to leadership failure. Leaders who fail to hack succession will fail to successfully position their organization for the future.

Many otherwise savvy business people don't understand succession as well as they would have you believe. They focus on optics, politics, and convenience more than on delivering the right outcome. Planning isn't the end game; it's the jumping off point. While succession is an issue at every level of an organization and for every position, nowhere is succession more important than at the top of the house.

With all eyeballs on Marissa Mayer at Yahoo! and Tim Cook at Apple, CEO succession is a hot topic these days—and rightly so. Few things adversely impact corporate culture, shareholder value, or brand equity like a failed CEO. Given the obvious importance of leadership from the top, what always amazes me is the ever-increasing turnover rate for chief executives. With the average tenure of Fortune 500 CEOs being less than five years, a company's board must always be thinking of succession. While departures are often unexpected, they should never be unplanned.

There is no arguing the fact failed chief executives can send a brand spiraling into decline, which can take years, or even decades, to recover from—if it recovers at all. In fact, the only thing I can think of worse than a failed CEO is a successive string of failed CEOs (e.g., HP—six CEOs since 1999 and Yahoo!—six CEOs since 2007). Contrast this with the fact that well-planned and properly executed CEO transitions can boost stakeholder confidence and drive an increase in stock price. It's a wonder more companies don't get this right.

Let me be clear—successions fail for one reason, and one reason only: a lack of leadership. Companies, boards, and their advisors who fail to successfully transition the CEO focus more on silly processes than the people and the culture. Put simply, these otherwise savvy business people don't understand succession as well as they would have you believe. They focus on optics, politics, and convenience more than delivering the right outcome. I've seen many corporate succession plans, and rarely does the readiness for succession match the readiness of the planning process.

As a result of my practice area emphasis, I normally find myself commencing work on 6 to 10 new Fortune 500 CEO succession engagements each year. This means at any given point in time I'm dealing with close to 20 companies in various stages of transitioning the chief executive. I've witnessed the best and worst of succession philosophies and practices, and I can assure you more companies get it wrong than right.

While most organizations have dealt with succession planning at some level, they rarely touch all the necessary constituencies with appropriate timing and care. Succession needs to be part of the values, vision, strategy, and culture of an organization. It must be embraced by leadership, communicated to the workforce, and understood by external stakeholders. It must be viewed as a step forward and not a regression. While many will overcomplicate succession, others tend to trivialize it. The truth is that succession is a blending of the art and science of leadership, people, positions, philosophies, relationships, culture, and a certainty of execution.

The complexity associated with succession is largely a result of the number of constituencies that must be addressed as a result of the process. Successful transitions become even more difficult when they are forced to occur on a short time frame because the proper planning failed to occur. Successful efforts address a minimum of the following 10 constituencies (in no particular order):

1. The board
2. The incoming CEO
3. The outgoing CEO
4. The executive leadership team
5. Internal candidates who didn't get the job
6. The workforce
7. The capital markets
8. Public policy
9. Customers, partners, vendors/suppliers
10. The media

The simple truth is that most companies can avoid the chaos and calamity associated with CEO succession failures by doing one thing well—hiring the right CEO to begin with. That said, selection must be followed by assimilation and then finally succession—three different phases with three different requirements.

Too many organizations simply botch the recruitment, selection, assimilation, and succession phases only to have to endure the entire cycle again. A failed CEO not only halts the momentum of the organization, but it sends a strong signal to the market that the board has been asleep at the wheel.

When succession fails, many will point the finger at the incoming or outgoing CEO, some will blame the HR team that failed to develop suitable internal candidates, and others will cast aspersions on the search firm that failed to deliver the right external candidate pool. While there's plenty of culpability to go around in any failed succession, people will often overlook the reality that the board of directors owns a great deal of the responsibility.

Having the right type of board composition and engagement will often be the key difference between a successful passing of the baton and a failed handoff. A disengaged board simply won't provide the proper amount of oversight and governance necessary to ensure succession becomes a cultural priority. Likewise, an overengaged board that crosses over the governance line into the management arena can do just as much damage to the process.

The board, as well as the subcommittees that oversee succession planning and selection, are the key to ensuring a successful CEO transition. If the board hasn't held the existing leadership team accountable for talent development and succession planning, they have simply failed in their oversight obligations. I'd suggest your organization keep the following three points in mind as you address succession:

1. **Internal vs. External:** Some will say if you have to go outside the enterprise to find a successor CEO, then succession has failed. This is utter rubbish—a myth, and a harmful one at that. All the leadership development programs in the world won't ensure that an internal candidate will be will be the right person for the job when it becomes available. The goal isn't to produce an internal candidate in a vacuum; the goal is to produce the right candidate at a given point in time—internal or external doesn't matter, it's finding the right candidate that matters. Successful transitions set internal candidates against external candidates to achieve the right outcome.

2. **Process versus People:** A plan doesn't succeed an outgoing leader; a person does. Succession requires more than planning, as plans don't develop people, but time, experience, and leaders do. Incoming leaders must do more than assume a leadership position or title; they must actually be willing to lead and capable of leading the organization through the present and into the future.

3. **Don't Pass the Buck:** Succession is not an HR problem—it's a leadership problem. At its essence, the succession of a CEO is complex collaboration between diverse constituencies. Succession is more than recruiting—hiring a successor candidate is not the solution, it's the beginning of the journey. Succession must be a cultural imperative aligned with the core values of the enterprise, or you'll be engaging in little more than a rolling of the dice.

Bottom line—organizations that make succession a priority are more successful than those that don't. Let me leave you with this quote from John Maxwell, "There is no success without a successor."

Final Thoughts

Leadership cannot flourish with small minds,
thinking about small things, in small ways.

I want you to recall something I noted earlier in the book—that leadership is a continuum and not a destination. It's never too late to start leading or commit to being a better leader. Ultimately, how you choose to lead and what you focus on is your choice, but I'd like to leave you with these final thoughts about what I consider to be the most important leadership hacks.

Like most of you, much has happened in my life over the past 18 months. My son returned from Afghanistan in one piece, and all of the men and women he led into combat returned alive. My son-in-law was accepted to medical school, I was blessed with three (soon to be four) new grandchildren, and my business and clients continued to prosper. Also during that time both my father and my mother-in-law passed away, and my wife had a major health scare. It's been a season of joy, a season of concern, and a season of loss. But most of all, it's been a time of reflection and growth.

Recent times have served to firmly confirm my belief that who you are remains infinitely more important than what you do. That the career successes you have, while nice, are fleeting and don't even begin to compare to the significance of those who build into your life on a regular and consistent basis. For that reason I want to encourage you to spend more time hacking your family life.

Hacking Your Family Life

I began my last book on the topic of family, and I'm choosing to start my final thoughts on family in this work. Over the years, I've come to believe there is only one surefire litmus test for measuring leadership success, and to the chagrin of many reading these words, it has little to do with what happens on the job. This topic might push a few buttons and test the boundaries of your comfort zone, but if you stick with me, I promise you'll be glad you did. I'm going to peel back the layers on your personal brand, question your priorities, and quite possibly put a big dent in your carefully crafted professional facade. We're about to get very personal—How's your family life?

If the opening paragraph of this section caused you to wince, then the text that follows is written just for you. If the next sentence seems a little preachy, it's meant to be. The true test of all leaders is not measured by what's accomplished in their professional life, but rather by what's accomplished at home. If you're a well-oiled machine at work, but your family is falling apart at the seams—who cares? Let me be blunt—you won't earn anyone's respect, at least not the respect of anyone who matters if your concern for career success overshadows your concern for the well-being of your family. If you're struggling with the family balance thing, my advice is simple: Don't attempt to balance your family—make them your priority.

The best leaders I know create a legacy that transcends their career. There are few things in life as thought provoking as witnessing what by all outward appearances seem to be successful executives, but as you begin to peel back the layers of their carefully crafted veneer, you quickly come to realize that they are little more than empty, bitter, and frustrated people. They work their entire careers chasing some illusive form of fulfillment only to fade into the sunset with nothing more than an empty lifetime of regrets as their reward.

I've simply lived too long to buy into the myth that success in the workplace will create happiness at home. While it makes for a nice sound bite to console those with a guilty conscience, *it is a lie*. If your business is growing, but your spouse is crying, and your children are neglected, it's time to do a reality check on your priorities. If your staff respects you, but your spouse doesn't, you have serious issues that need your immediate attention. If you would rather spend time with your online "friends" than with your children, it's time to pull the ripcord on your Internet connection.

Here's the cold hard truth—if you cheat your family to invest in your career, you and your loved ones will pay a very heavy price. It is simply wrong to value your workplace commitments over your family commitments—moreover, it's not necessary. If the focus is on your family, your career won't suffer, it will flourish. Get this wrong, and not only will your family suffer, but so will you as you someday mourn the loss of what could have been, but cannot be recovered.

If you really want to get to know me, don't waste time reading my bio or scrutinizing my professional successes and failures, get to know my wife and my children. My best work, the work that I'm most proud of, is the relationship I have with the love of my life whom I've been married to for almost three decades, and with my two grown children who now consistently teach me more about life than I taught them.

While I've had more career success than I probably deserve, I'm just as flawed as anyone reading this text. That said, I don't regret a single second of time I've invested in my family, but I've lost track of all the regrets I have over time spent away from my family.

You see, everyone creates a legacy—the question is, will it be one worth leaving? While a legacy is classically defined as something of significant and/or lasting value that survives its creator, the best legacy is one that can be lived before it is left behind.

The bottom line is this: If you're a superstar at work, but a slacker at home, you're not succeeding at anything other than being a disingenuous, egocentric charlatan. If this describes you, you're not a leader; you are a poser. As a very wise person once said (my wife), "Don't waste your time investing in those who won't be crying at your funeral."

Family deserves your attention, but as a leader you cannot afford apathy at any level. Truly successful leaders know they cannot just go through the motions, just phone it in, or just check the boxes.

Hacking Apathy

Everyone reading this book should take this next statement to heart—*stop checking boxes*. To believe leadership can be reduced to task management is simply flawed thinking. Here's the thing—you can manage to a list, but you certainly cannot lead to a list. A check-the-box approach to leadership accomplishes only one thing—it limits your ability to lead.

Leadership isn't about checking boxes. Great leadership thrives beyond typical borders and constraints—it lives outside the norm. Leadership requires more than just going through the motions. Real leaders reshape, reinvent, or remove boxes, but they refuse to simply check them.

True leadership doesn't reveal itself by meeting expectations; it shows itself by exceeding them. Leadership looks past the obvious, beyond the optics, and it embraces the challenge of seeking the extraordinary. Leadership is demonstrated by having the courage to do more than just go through the motions.

Think about it like this—do you want to be a leader who simply does what's expected, or do you want to be a leader who makes *what if* a reality? Let me say this as simply as I can: Leaders don't settle—they move forward. They innately stretch themselves, as well as those they lead. The best leaders don't have a maintenance mind-set. They focus their efforts on discovery, creation, improvement, disruption, and growth.

Think of the best leader you know; now think of the best leaders throughout history—did any of the leaders who came to mind make an impact by just checking the box? The next time you're tempted to check a box, consider asking yourself the following questions: Is this the best I can do? Am I leading or am I settling? Are those whom I lead better off as a result of this decision?

Checking a box is an easy thing to do, but that doesn't mean it's the right thing to do—it doesn't make you a leader. Just as checking boxes provides an easy way out so does making excuses.

Hacking the Excuse Gap

Leaders don't offer, nor do they accept excuses. True leadership demands the character to demonstrate personal responsibility for one's actions, and the courage to hold others accountable for theirs. Excuses attempt to conceal personal or professional insecurities, laziness, and/ or lack of ability. They accomplish nothing but to distract, dilute, and deceive. It was Benjamin Franklin who said, "He that is good for making excuses is seldom good for anything else."

The word *excuse* is most commonly defined as a reason or explanation put forward to defend or justify a fault or offense. History's greatest leaders have always fostered cultures of commitment, trust, and performance, where action is valued over rhetoric. Leaders who issue or accept excuses are complicit to muting performance and fueling mediocrity.

The problem we face as a society is we live in a time where the person with the best excuses wins. Excuses have become the rule, and performance has become the exception—a sad commentary to be sure. However the solution is a rather simple one—I've always said that people will stop offering excuses the minute those in positions of leadership stop accepting them.

People have overcome poverty, drug addiction, incarceration, abuse, divorce, mental illness, victimization, and virtually every challenge known to man. Life is full of examples of the uneducated, the mentally and physically challenged, people born into war-torn impoverished backgrounds, who could have made excuses, but who instead chose a different path—they chose to overcome the odds and succeed.

John Wooden said, "Never make excuses. Your friends won't accept them and your foes won't believe them." The great thing about performance is that it obviates the necessity of an explanation. In these troubled times, inept leaders blame their business woes on the economy, while skilled leaders find a way to thrive. Challenges and setbacks are opportunities for growth and development, not permission space for rationalizations and justifications. The best leaders not only understand this, they ensure the entirety of their organization practices it.

Here's the thing—sane people don't expect perfection from leaders, but they do expect leaders to be transparent and accountable. Accepting responsibility for your actions, or the actions of your team makes you honorable and trustworthy—it also humanizes you. People don't want the talking head of a politician for a leader, they want someone they can connect to, and relate with. They not only want someone they trust, but someone who trusts them as well.

One of my favorite quotes is by Edward R. Murrow: "Difficulty is the excuse history never accepts." The fastest way to lose respect as a leader is to focus on optics over ethics. If you're more concerned about political fallout than solving the problem, you have failed as a leader. Even though responsibility for decisions defaults to the leader, responsibility should be a thing of design, not default. It should be readily accepted and not easily denied—this is real leadership.

The collective goal underpinning the construction of the prior 11 chapters is to use leadership hacks to enable a culture of leadership. Nobody argues the importance of culture, but there is great debate about which constructs must be present in order to create the right cultural dynamics. In my experience, the only sustainable culture worthy of building is a culture of leadership. When you become fluent in hacking leadership, you'll have set the foundation for building a true culture of leadership that will attract and retain the right talent, encourage the right actions, and deliver the needed outcomes.

Think about this for a moment—with all our experience and all the research, with all the resources and all the focus on leadership, do you find it perplexing, if not altogether disturbing, that our world has never been more lacking for true leaders? Casual observation might lead you to conclude leadership has devolved rather than evolved. If you pay close attention to the media and world events, it would appear that those serving themselves greatly outnumber those who place service above self. Here's the thing—we'll never all agree on what leadership is, or is not, but I think most reasonable people will concur it's time for a change.

In the final analysis leadership is less about structure and more about vision and philosophy. Nothing inspires change and innovation like great leadership, and likewise, there is no more costly legacy system to maintain than poor leadership.

Put simply, the greatest testimony to the power of real leadership is what happens in its absence—very little.

I wish you the best of luck on your leadership journey.

About the Author

MIKE MYATT is the CEO at N2growth, a global leader in providing leadership development services to Fortune 500 companies. He is widely regarded as America's Top CEO Coach, is the author of *Leadership Matters*, and is a *Forbes* Leadership Columnist.

Mike Myatt is one of the world's most respected authorities on leadership, having been recognized by Thinkers50 and other organizations as one of today's preeminent leadership thinkers. He is a Senior Fellow at the Gordian Institute, and his theories and practices have been taught at many of the nation's top business schools.

Mr. Myatt has worked directly with more than 150 public company CEOs, and his representative corporate clients include AT&T, Bank of America, Deloitte, EMC, Humana, IBM, JPMorgan Chase, McGraw-Hill, Merrill Lynch, PepsiCo, and other leading global brands.

Mr. Myatt also frequently lectures and keynotes on the topics of leadership and problem solving. If you're interested in contacting him, you can e-mail him at info@n2growth.com or follow him on Twitter @mikemyatt.

More information on Mike Myatt can be found on his company website, www.n2growth.com.

Index